# THE BASICS OF
# INVESTING

## Gerald Krefetz

Dearborn
Financial Publishing, Inc.

While a great deal of care has been taken to provide accurate and current information, the ideas, suggestions, general principles and conclusions presented in this text are subject to local, state and federal laws and regulations, court cases and any revisions of same. The reader is thus urged to consult legal counsel regarding any points of law—this publication should not be used as a substitute for competent legal advice.

Publisher: Kathleen A. Welton
Associate Editor: Karen A. Christensen
Senior Project Editor: Jack L. Kiburz
Interior Design: Lucy Jenkins
Cover Design: Sam Concialdi

Published by Dearborn Financial Publishing, Inc.

Printed in the United States of America

94  10  9  8  7  6  5  4  3

**Library of Congress Cataloging-in-Publication Data**

Krefetz, Gerald.
    The basics of investing / Gerald Krefetz.
        p.  cm. — (Making the most of your money series)
    Includes index.
    ISBN 0-79310-358-4 (paper)
        1. Investments   2. Finance, Personal.   I. Title.   II. Series:
    Krefetz, Gerald. Making the most of your money series.
HG4521.K7    1992                                          91–42811
332.6'78—dc20                                              CIP

# Dedication

*To Dorothy, Nadine and Adriene*

# Contents

# *Introduction*

## WHAT THIS BOOK WILL DO FOR YOU

The purpose of this book, and the three that follow in this series, is to provide you with practical and usable information about your money—the money you now have and the funds you will undoubtedly accumulate. It will attempt to move you through the financial passages of life. This trip should not be compared to climbing an insurmountable mountain, but rather to a journey on a bus or train. You get off at the stop where you feel most comfortable, the one most appropriate for your personal situation, both now and in the foreseeable future.

The first book in the series will lead you to some fundamental decisions about what to do with your money:

- How much should you have in savings before you think about investing? And what are the best ways for you to save your money?
- What are the goals of investing? Which goal or combination of goals is right for you at this stage of your life? And should you rethink your goals?
- How comfortable are you with taking chances with money? Are you risk-averse? Risk-neutral? Risk-loving?

- What investment alternatives are currently appropriate for you—in light of your present investment goals and your attitude toward risk?
- Should you undertake to manage your own investment program, or should you entrust the day-to-day management of that program to someone else?
- How should you go about setting up an investment portfolio that reflects your goals?
- What steps should you take to monitor your investments and shift your funds when your goals or external circumstances change?

Once you have answered these basic questions, you will, in effect, have sketched out in broad strokes an investment plan that needs to be fleshed out and implemented. It is at this point that the remaining three books in the series can be of real help:

- *The Basics of Stocks* will show you how to get started on a program of investing in stocks and how to monitor that program to maximize your opportunities for profits.
- *The Basics of Bonds* will guide you through the complexities of the fixed-income market and help you set up and monitor an effective program of investing in bonds and other fixed-interest instruments.
- *The Basics of Speculating* will lead you through the most speculative investment opportunities for high growth as well as the risks and pitfalls.

In short, the entire series is designed to lead you through a decision-making process that will produce a custom-tailored savings and investment plan right for you, given your own assessment of your needs, dreams and goals.

You must, however, be prepared for detours and round-abouts because the future remains unknown and unknowable. At best you can plan only on the basis of partial information and uncertain assumptions. Thus it is important to be flexible and to reassess both your trip plan and your actions on a periodic basis.

Change, of course, is one of the basic laws of life. The transition from one stage to another means frequent reexamination of your goals and your means of achieving them. Therefore, there can be no one permanent solution or one answer to your financial concerns. Those concerns and problems are always changing. Moreover, there are different paths to get you to the same location. This book will assist you in moving from one crossroads to another.

## WHAT THIS BOOK WON'T DO FOR YOU

Having now told you what this book *will* do for you, it is also important to tell you—in the name of full disclosure—what this book *will not* do for you. It will not make you popular, powerful, famous or an instant millionaire. Putting your funds to work profitably is a careful and disciplined business; it should not be rushed. If anyone tells you it's "the last one available" or that "this opportunity is a once-in-a-lifetime chance," a red light should immediately go on in your head. In the financial world greed is the enemy of good sense. Remember, if you don't understand it (whether it is the penalty provisions for cashing in a certificate of deposit before maturity or the prospectus of a new stock issue) stay away from it. Don't be gullible and don't be panicked. In the words of an old saw, "Act in haste and repent at leisure."

You will not be presented with complicated formulas to boggle your mind and make your eyes glaze over. Successful personal money management requires little more than some simple calculations. This book is free of economic jargon or abstract financial terms. Only practical and down-to-earth information—and how to apply it—is included. There are no magic investment recipes that have met the test of time, for if such recipes were successful for a short term, they would cease to work in the long term as news about the system got out and everyone started to use them.

In short, there are no magic formulations to make you immediately wealthy. There are, however, effective methods of saving and investing, but there are no secrets about them. They succeed because of common sense and diligent application. This book details some of the ways of making and accumulating money—methods that have worked in good times and bad and that should work for you.

Nothing in this book should confuse or confound you. It is based on the premise that anything that cannot be explained in simple, straightforward English probably is not worth examining, let alone is it a safe depository for your serious money.

Conservation of money should be a paramount concern to everyone who works for a living or is lucky enough to have inherited a windfall. Money in the bank, or any other kind of financial asset, increases your freedom of action and your ability to choose—whether it be a job, a place to live or a college education for your children. Knowledge makes you free, but so too does a surplus of funds. Only through a regular and systematic plan for saving and investing can you hope to achieve independence and freedom. Risks may lie in the most conservative of plans, but prudence and common sense can limit those risks.

# • 1 •

## *Why Run the Risk of Investing?*

If you are frustrated by the incessant hype of competitive financial services and are fearful of missteps and mistakes that can do irreparable damage to savings, you may well wonder whether it's even worth your while to get involved. The stock market crash in October 1987 and the fall in the fixed-income market in the spring of that year were both riveting and disturbing events.

Nevertheless, these events must be kept in perspective. In 1987 Standard & Poor's 500 stock average finished the year up 5 percent over 1986, and the bond market went down by a similar amount, while the average yield on long-term bonds for that year was more than 9 percent. The five-year bull market (1982–87) saw Standard & Poor's 500 advance by more than 200 percent. Long-term investors—the kind that make the highest returns—had enviable results, the October "meltdown" notwithstanding.

Long-term investors made further gains in 1988 and 1989. The stock market extended the bull market, making the boom one of the longest in history. Two years after the meltdown, the market was up approximately 1,000 points on the Dow Jones Industrial Average. Standard & Poor's 500 had an annual return of approximately 20 percent from 1984 through 1989. The bond market also rose as interest rates came down.

The long-term saver also had good news. Starting in 1980, a depositor could have had access to extraordinarily safe returns—more than 8 percent for U.S. series EE savings bonds to occasional double-digit returns in money market deposit accounts.

It is important for savers and investors to take a long perspective in dealing with financial matters. Traders and speculators must be concerned with the daily fluctuations of markets, but it is counterproductive for you to worry over the daily ups and downs of the stock exchanges and the money markets. Solid gains in the financial world are almost always associated with holding long-term positions. The idea is to get rich slowly, but surely.

## WHY IS SAVING NOT ENOUGH?

It is a profound mistake to assume that conservation of money means putting money in the most secure account or safest depository. French peasants kept their gold coins in wool socks under the mattress or buried in their backyards. While it might have been a wise move for the French, considering their history of revolution, devaluation and invasion, it makes less sense for modern Americans. Protection of funds in the most conservative way can be disastrous in a period of inflation.

Remember, though the government was dedicated to suppressing inflation throughout the 1980s, the consumer price index (CPI) rose an average of 5 percent per year. Your 1980 dollar was worth only about half in terms of purchasing power in 1990. It would be naive to expect the 1990s to be any different.

To put it more strongly: Locking funds up in sterile safe-deposit boxes or low-interest accounts defeats the purpose of accumulating money. Inflation does its secret work by devaluing your purchasing power when you are not looking. In short, the total avoidance of risk earlier in life guarantees a loss of real buying power later. This can be illustrated by looking at a few figures. If you had $5,000 in your safe-deposit box at the start of 1981, you would still have $5,000 on January 1, 1992. If you had $5,000 in a passbook savings account paying 5.5 percent at your local bank (guaranteed by the Federal Deposit Insurance Corporation, or FDIC), you would have had approximately $9,010 at the end of the period.

In effect, your $9,010 was worth only $4,505. Not only did you fall behind with your money in the bank's passbook account, but you still had to pay taxes on the 5.5 percent interest the bank paid. If you paid taxes at the 28 percent marginal tax bracket, your savings were earning, after taxes, 3.96 percent, and in the 15 percent tax bracket, only 4.68 percent. Each year your funds fell further behind in purchasing power. You would have needed a considerably higher yield to have remained even—that is, to counteract the depreciation of your funds.

Thus, the return on a riskless investment was lower than on one with some risk. Paradoxically, the riskless investment left the individual poorer and, in the final analysis, less able to contend with the ups and downs of daily existence. Riskless investors or savers may feel better away from the volatility of the business world, but over the long haul their savings and assets invisibly erode.

A prudent approach is not necessarily ultraconservative, but it is one that recognizes definable risk and plans to take advantage or profit thereby. There are times to be aggressive and times to be cautious. Your mix of funds is forever changing, partially because of the passing of financial stages and partially because of the changing economic environment. If you recognize that prudence does not mean hunkering down in a bunker but rather acting on reasonable expectations that allow for diversified savings and investments, you can have the best of both worlds.

An investment program can help increase the value of savings faster if undertaken early and pursued consistently. Even passive investors, those who let other people do their investing, are likely to outperform savings bank passbook rates by 50 or 100 percent. Growth of assets at those levels will sharply reduce the time it takes to acquire a down payment on a home, build a college tuition fund or gather a nest egg for retirement.

## A THREE-LEGGED FINANCIAL PLAN

Few of us ever have enough money. The purpose of saving and investing is not to make you immediately rich so that you will forever have enough money—an unrealistic idea—but to build additional funds in a slow but sure manner. Whether it be for present consumption or future plans, extra money is always welcome.

It is shortsighted to start investing without substantial money in the bank, funds that you will not touch even in the most dire circumstances or, conversely, in a more propitious investment climate when you are tempted to bet the ranch.

Since savings come in different forms, it is worthwhile to review different savings programs, how to calculate interest rates and yields, appropriate savings vehicles for the short and long term and the level of savings at your stage of life that you might reasonably achieve before moving on to build an investment program. You might consider your world of money akin to a three-legged milk stool.

## Involuntary Savings

The first leg is involuntary savings. These are funds set aside to pay certain fixed expenses. Some of those debt payments are a form of saving, though the actual cash value may not be apparent for many years. For example, mortgage payments initially go to paying down the interest charges with but a small fraction to amortize the principal. As a mortgage ages, the reverse occurs—most of the payment goes for principal and a declining amount to interest charges.

Other involuntary savings are found in life insurance policies (all but term insurance) as the "inside buildup" subsequently has a cash value. The same is true of income savings plans, payroll savings plans and pension plans. Involuntary savings provide a steady and sure way to build assets and, equally important, are a source of borrowable funds for education, medical emergencies and retirement.

## Voluntary Savings

Voluntary savings, the second leg, are harder to come by. In 1991 Americans saved only 4 percent of their disposable income. There are no secrets to saving money: the only thing needed is willpower. It is generally agreed that one's assets should ideally increase about 10 percent yearly. You should manage to save 5 percent of your disposable income, the amount left over after you have finished paying routine bills. Better yet, a worthwhile goal is to save 5 percent of your total income. This of course is difficult early in life when you are faced with large expenditures to start a career and/or raise a family.

### Your Investment Program

The third leg of the stool is your investment program. The one place where it is possible to increase the return on your assets at an average rate that historically surpasses interest rates paid by banks and other borrowers is in financial assets (see Table 1.1).

Investing—whether in stocks, bonds or hard assets—is the only way to achieve real growth. The one constant we can all be sure of is inflation. Thus money saved in the bank, after taxes, remains almost static in absolute terms but is being constantly eroded in terms of its purchasing power. Governments have a long tradition of expropriating one's savings by means of the twin pincers of inflation and taxation. Unhappily, the sea of red ink facing the nation in the last decade of the twentieth century virtually dictates that there will be no relief from these two invidious forces.

## WHAT ARE THE RISKS OF INVESTING?

There are, to be sure, some risks in investing whether in the stock or bond markets. These risks were brought home in the major crash of October 1987 and in the smaller crash of October 1989. Some individuals did indeed lose money; however, most investors did not—especially the ones who refused to panic.

Free markets at times become overpriced and under-priced. They tend to correct these exaggerations or abuses. Sometimes corrections take place in a day or two, as they did on October 19 and 20 of 1987, but they often take months to work out these corrections.

In the October 1987 meltdown, the fall was dramatic and frightening, as the stock market lost about a third of its value in a few days. We need not go into all the reasons for

**TABLE 1.1**   Investment Performance

Salomon Brothers publishes an annual study tracking investment returns for a wide range of assets. The following are compound annual returns, including dividend or interest income, for the periods ended June 1, 1991.

|  | 20 Years | | 10 Years | | 5 Years | | 1 Year | |
|---|---|---|---|---|---|---|---|---|
|  | *Return* | *Rank* | *Return* | *Rank* | *Return* | *Rank* | *Return* | *Rank* |
| Old masters | 12.32% | 1 | 15.84% | 2 | 23.36% | 1 | 6.53% | 5 |
| Stocks | 11.65 | 2 | 16.03 | 1 | 13.33 | 3 | 11.77 | 3 |
| Chinese ceramics | 11.59 | 3 | 8.07 | 5 | 15.12 | 2 | 3.64 | 8 |
| Gold | 11.50 | 4 | −2.89 | 12 | 0.98 | 12 | − 0.73 | 12 |
| Diamonds | 10.46 | 5 | 6.38 | 6 | 10.23 | 4 | 0.00 | 11 |
| Stamps | 10.03 | 6 | −0.73 | 10 | −2.43 | 13 | − 7.67 | 13 |
| Bonds | 9.35 | 7 | 15.15 | 3 | 9.66 | 5 | 13.20 | 2 |
| Oil | 8.85 | 8 | −5.92 | 13 | 8.50 | 6 | 20.66 | 1 |
| 3-month Treasury bills | 8.62 | 9 | 8.79 | 4 | 7.02 | 7 | 7.13 | 4 |
| Housing | 7.27 | 10 | 4.37 | 7 | 4.55 | 9 | 4.70 | 7 |
| Consumer price index | 6.29 | 11 | 4.30 | 8 | 4.52 | 10 | 5.04 | 6 |
| U.S. farmland | 6.25 | 12 | −1.81 | 11 | 1.28 | 11 | 2.10 | 9 |
| Silver | 4.99 | 13 | −9.27 | 14 | −4.80 | 14 | −18.87 | 14 |
| Foreign exchange | 4.49 | 14 | 3.61 | 9 | 5.44 | 8 | 0.24 | 10 |

SOURCE: ©Salomon Brothers Inc. 1991.

the market collapse, but certainly stock prices had risen to unsustainable heights. In brief, shares became overvalued when measured by historical standards.

One other important factor helped contribute to the fall: computerized trading programs helped to trigger the selloff. These automatic trades set off a descending spiral of market activity that fed on itself.

Computerized trading programs have now been curbed, though not eliminated from the stock market. Perhaps the fluctuations in the future will be less dramatic, but the higher the market goes, the greater the number of points it is likely to move.

Anyone who bought shares shortly before the selloff obviously had a loss immediately after the crash. It must be remembered, however, that most investors emerged unscathed. That is especially true of the long-term investor. Anyone who had bought a well-rounded portfolio at the beginning of the bull market in 1982 would have doubled his or her money by the end of 1987. In fact, the general market averages for 1987 show not a loss but a gain of more than 4 percent for the whole year.

The risk was *not* in the securities, most of which proved to be perfectly sound holdings. The risk was in selling out in a state of panic.

There are a number of different kinds of risks in the financial world—market risk, interest rate risk, company risk and political risk, among others—but the greatest risk is acting precipitously and out of fear.

Markets, as J.P. Morgan noted, will fluctuate, as they always have. If witnessing the contracting and expanding of your investments has a depressing or frightening affect on you, perhaps you should not be directly involved with the stock or bond markets. Instead, consider less volatile vehicles, such as mutual funds, or simply designate a professional investment manager to take charge of your investment funds. There is no reason you cannot master the basic fundamentals of the markets. On the other hand, there is no reason to participate in an activity that causes anxiety and may be dangerous to your wealth. Passive investors can still benefit from the investment process without exposing themselves to undue risks.

In the final analysis, investing for the long term can be a very positive contribution to your personal wealth. It can raise the return on your invested funds by 50 or 100 percent over most savings vehicles. But first it is important to establish a level of savings necessary to support an investment program.

# • 2 •

## *How Much Should You Have in Savings before You Invest?*

Under normal circumstances you should not seriously consider investing unless you satisfy at least one of the three following conditions:

1. You have one year's income or $20,000 (whichever is greater) deposited in a bank or in some other form of savings.
2. Your current assets equal or exceed twice your current liabilities.
3. You have just acquired a sudden windfall or inheritance, which should be thought of as capital and not as current income.

Some observers suggest that it is already too late if you wait to meet these criteria. They would urge you to start an active investment program as early as an active savings program. Indeed, they view both as part and parcel of modern money management techniques. Perhaps this is true, but, realistically, most people are not psychologically ready to invest until they feel financially secure. And security for most people is money in the bank.

***How Much Cash or Cash Equivalent Should You Keep on Hand?*** While there can never be too much of a good thing, excessive cash or cash equivalent (money

9

market mutual fund shares; Treasury bills, etc.) indicates that it could be put to more productive use. Have sufficient cash to cover three months' living expenses.

*How Is Your Cash or Cash Equivalent Employed?* An incredible amount of funds are left in savings bank (S&L) passbook or statement savings accounts earning minimum interest. Since deregulation of financial markets in the 1980s, the savings industry now competes by offering a variety of accounts that produce more than basic passbook interest. Thus, it is possible to receive higher yields within the same insured bank. When possible, cash savings should be deposited in a money market bank account or money market mutual fund to capture market-driven interest rates. Commit to saving 5 percent of your annual earnings: $25,000 requires placing $1,250 into savings and $50,000 means $2,500. This is a high percentage to save, and some individuals may be able to save only 5 percent of disposable income, that is, after they have paid their bills.

## HOW FAST SHOULD YOUR ASSETS GROW?

Individuals should protect themselves by putting in place a mandatory saving and investment plan. Theoretically, it would be nice to see net assets increase by 10 percent a year. The first step is to save at least 5 percent of your total income, or at least 5 percent of your disposable income. The median family income in the late Eighties was $31,000 according to the Census Bureau, while the highest family income, $40,000, belonged to the 45-to-54 age group. If 5 percent was saved annually, the results over time would look like Table 2.1.

**TABLE 2.1**    5 Percent Annual Savings of Earned Income
Compounded Daily at 6 Percent

| Income | 1st Year | 2nd Year | 5th Year | 10th Year | 20th Year | 30th Year |
|---|---|---|---|---|---|---|
| $31,000 | $1,550 | $3,193 | $ 8,737 | $20,430 | $57,083 | $122,540 |
| $40,000 | $2,000 | $4,120 | $11,274 | $26,362 | $73,572 | $158,116 |

The calculation in Table 2.1 assumes no increase in salary. Even on that basis, a modest 5 percent annual saving of your earnings at 6 percent can produce healthy six-figure savings.

There are no hard-and-fast rules about saving—it certainly depends on your personal economic conditions, your temperament and of course the unsuspected demands that inevitably arise. How much you save depends on your age, family situation (or lack of it) and your path. If you are paying off student loans for five or ten years after college or graduate school, your net worth is not likely to increase rapidly, if at all. And certainly a new family and a new home, both items of great cost, are likely to keep your accumulation curve relatively flat.

In the final analysis, how much you save depends on how much you earn, and that of course changes throughout life. Nevertheless, it is important to establish a regular savings habit for your own financial health. Savings are initially the basic component of your total assets. After a number of years your assets will grow from the interest on your savings and the growth of your investments.

If your savings grow at no less than 5 percent a year, how fast will your assets grow? That of course depends on the rate of interest paid on savings, both for short-term and long-term deposits. As a rule, a 10 percent annual increase of net worth might reasonably be expected—half based on new savings and the other half based on interest on previous savings (approximately 5 percent), as well as the paydown on mortgages and other asset-building debts.

## SAVINGS PATTERNS

The Greeks thought there were three distinct phases of a person's life, the great Asian religious leaders thought there were four and Shakespeare suggested seven stages of life. Today one's lifespan is longer, career and work experiences are more varied, educational requirements are extended and marital life is uncertain, with frequent second marriages. All these factors increase the number of stages experienced in life. Varied life-styles indicate that people choose some stages, but not others. Therefore, the situations that follow are meant to show some possible savings alternatives, but they are not mandatory progressions. You pay your money and you make your choices—nothing is written in stone and there are no "correct" ways of saving.

There are examples of savings plans that are designed to provide you with the highest return and maximum flexibility. Be aware that there is a trade-off between the two. Institutions such as banks and savings and loan companies pay the highest interest for money that they can in turn commit for long periods to their borrowers.

However, it is disastrous in the banking business to lend funds on a long-term basis and borrow them from depositors on a short-term basis. Bankers try to avoid this dilemma by promising not only to pay more for long-term funds but to penalize depositors who remove their funds before maturity or due dates. Thus, place your funds in long-term time deposits to obtain the best rates of interest—often 2, 3 or 4 percent more than the rates provided for short-term deposits. There are times when short-term interest rates may be higher than long-term ones. This inversion of yields is relatively rare and savers cannot easily take advantage of it. However, investors in the fixed-income market and bonds should be aware of this condition to make a profit.

On the other hand, you need short-term savings for specific calls on your money to meet medical emergencies, educational payments, vacation trips, car payments, moving expenses and all the other frequent planned and unplanned expenses of living. At a minimum you should keep 12 weeks' reserve (of your ordinary expenses) of cash in short-term savings before committing funds to longer-term accounts. Finally, everyone needs transaction funds— money you do not expect to sit in a bank for more than a few weeks, or until you get around to paying routine bills. Depending on your personal circumstances, the following arrangements provide high yield and flexibility:

*From Birth to Age 14.*   Under the new tax code, there is no benefit to saving in children's names. However, to encourage saving, youngsters should have their own passbook savings accounts.

Interest earnings above $1,000 are taxed to parents.

*From Age 14 to a Full-time Job.*   All earnings are now taxed to the adolescent; therefore, it pays to save at his or her lower tax rate. Keep the passbook account and open a regular checking account at a savings bank that does not charge a monthly maintenance fee.

*From a Full-time Job to a Spouse.*   Switch from passbook to statement savings for more businesslike accounting. For long-term savings, have your employer arrange to buy U.S. savings bonds with a minimum 6 percent interest rate but with an adjustable rate (after five years) tied to U.S. Treasury auctions. Check on credit union membership for cheaper banking facilities if available.

*From a Spouse to a Family.* Open a joint family checking account, preferably a Negotiable Order of Withdrawal (NOW) account if both husband and wife work. Switch from a statement savings to a money market deposit account to take advantage of higher yields without tying up funds.

*From a Family to a First Home.* Consolidate all bank accounts in one institution in preparation for taking out a mortgage to improve your bargaining position. Consider buying five-year certificates of deposit (CDs) with long-term savings, gifts and inheritances to obtain a bank's best rates. Some banks offer passbook loans where you borrow your own money: the net result lowers the cost of a loan.

*From a First Home to a First Business.* Keep separate checking accounts for home expenses and business or professional expenses, even if the business is in your home. Borrow funds from the bank, collateralized against your assets, to start a new business. For example, home interest costs are partially deductible, whereas if you use your own funds, you lose their earnings.

*From a First Business to Retirement.* If you are employed, maximize your contributions to a salary reduction plan. If self-employed, use individual retirement accounts, (IRAs), Keoghs, and simplified employee pension (SEP) tax-deferred savings accounts to buy CDs and U.S. Treasury bonds. Convert Series EE U.S. savings bonds to Series HH, which provide for periodic interest payments semiannually. Consider an annuity to increase savings after retirement.

*Senior Citizen.* Harvest retirement plans and apply for Social Security. Keep your life insurance in force and consider borrowing against its cash value for emergencies. Look into reverse home mortgages, where banks provide for monthly payments in return for the ownership of your house. Make sure all bank accounts are jointly owned with a right-of-survivor clause. To avoid lengthy probate, ask your attorney about a living trust (which bypasses the surrogate's court).

Whatever you earn, attempt to save 5 percent of your disposable income, at the very least. But savings should be tied to your age and your career. As your net worth increases, savings will come both from active earnings and passive income, such as dividends and interest. In the early years of a career, 5 percent may be difficult to achieve, but at the end of a career, 15 percent may be too little. If you have difficulty with voluntary savings, consider a form of forced savings, such as insurance, a retirement account or payroll deduction. In a land where consumption is a way of life, it is difficult to save.

### Y·O·U·R   M·O·V·E

- When your passbook account reaches $1,000, consider other demand deposit accounts that pay higher rates of interest, or consider a time deposit account.
- Virtually all banks, savings and loan companies and credit unions offer money market deposit accounts that pay higher rates of interest without tying up your funds for a long period of time. But check to see if there is a limit as to the number of checks that may be drawn on a monthly basis.
- Place most of your savings in three-year to five-year time deposits, such as CDs, to obtain the highest rates of interest. The balance of your savings should be kept

in cash or equivalents (money market funds) to meet small emergencies.

- Keep transaction funds in a checking account—one that preferably pays interest. Negotiable Order of Withdrawal accounts (NOW and Super NOW) pay interest on demand deposits. While there may be a minimum balance required, you can write any number of checks without being penalized.

- Savers with larger sums may wish to enter into an arrangement with a bank for a repurchase agreement. The bank sells you an interest in U.S. securities it owns and agrees to buy it back at a later date at a predetermined higher price. This is *not* an insured bank deposit, though the risk is minimal.

- Make sure your savings are insured by the FDIC or the National Credit Union Share Insurance Fund. Federal deposit insurance is superior to state insurance schemes. In general, each account is insured up to $100,000. If you have more than one account in a bank and the accounts exceed $100,000 combined, check with the institution for the exact amount of insurance coverage.

- Save at the highest compound interest rates available for the greatest return on your funds. Remember that 5 percent of an average salary of $31,000 is $1,550. If you saved only that every year for 30 years at 5 percent, you would have $122,540 before taxes.

# • 3 •

# *What Are the Best Ways for You To Save?*

Everyone's investment path starts with savings. Even though there is a wider horizon to personal money management, you may well decide that substantial savings programs are sufficient for your needs. You should be aware of other strategies that go beyond savings. A number of these investment techniques will be discussed later in this book, but you are under no mandatory obligation to pursue them if you feel content with a well-established savings program.

## WHAT TYPES OF SAVINGS ACCOUNTS CAN YOU USE?

Here is a brief review of the common types of savings accounts available at most banks.

- *Regular savings accounts.* These standard passbook accounts are demand accounts. That means your funds are available at any time. There no longer are limitations on the rates of interest that may be paid on these accounts, but 5.5 percent is the norm. Commercial banks sometimes pay less.

- *Statement savings accounts.* To automate, banks have encouraged passbook holders to switch to statement accounts. These demand accounts pay the same rate of interest as passbook accounts, and earnings are posted monthly.
- *Money market deposit accounts.* These are also demand accounts. Rates of interest, however, fluctuate and are subject to change monthly, if not more frequently. While the rates are the highest of all demand accounts, there may be an interest rate penalty if your monthly balance falls below the initial minimum, which is typically $1,000 to $2,500. Some banks limit the number of withdrawals per month and assess a steep penalty for any additional withdrawals.
- *Time deposits.* Short-term time accounts (7 to 31 days) have fixed maturity dates, and there may be penalties for early withdrawal, though additional funds can be added at any time. Interest rates are fixed when these accounts start. Short-term time deposits have relatively low rates of interest.
- *Certificates of deposit (CDs).* These certificates most commonly run from 6 to 60 months. Interest rates are fixed at the start and do not fluctuate. The minimum deposit in a CD is $500, and a substantial penalty is levied for early withdrawal.
- *Special-purpose certificates of deposit.* Some banks offer designer certificates that are customized for specific needs. Other banks issue CDs that are linked to stock exchange indices, thus offering either a fixed rate of interest and/or some percentage of market gains. Some banks offer CDs tied to an index of college costs to keep abreast of educational expenses.
- *Negotiable Orders of Withdrawal (NOW and Super NOW).* NOW accounts are forms of demand checking accounts, which pay 5 or 5.5 percent on balances. A minimum balance of $1,000 to $2,500 is usually

required. Super NOWs carry a higher rate of interest but require larger initial balances. If the minimum initial balance is violated, the rate falls to that of the simple NOW.

Short-term saving is better than not saving at all, but banks reserve their lowest rates of interest for short-term savers or money-on-demand deposits. Thus you should keep only small sums in these accounts for ordinary expenses. Conversely, banks pay their best rates for long-term time deposits. Your serious money should be put in these accounts, since they will not only earn the best returns, but you will also be discouraged from invading them.

## HOW DO INTEREST RATES COMPARE?

Interest rates change from bank to bank, and just as important, they are calculated by different formulas. In general the highest interest rate, combined with daily compounding from day of deposit to day of withdrawal, results in the highest yields to the depositor. But be aware that some banks compound daily, monthly, quarterly, semiannually or annually, while others pay only simple interest. To further complicate matters, some banks use average balances, some calculate at the start of the month, some at the end of the period and some use a combination to arrive at the principal upon which interest is based.

Besides obtaining the highest rate of interest, make sure you also obtain an account that is compounded as frequently as possible, preferably daily. While the difference between simple interest and compound interest is not dramatic, the following calculations show that compound interest does put more money in your account:

- $500 at a simple 6 percent interest for five years is $669.
- $500 at a daily compound interest of 6 percent for five years is $678.

Most people bank by convenient location. It may pay you to save at banks, thrifts or credit unions that are not so convenient but provide higher yields. On the other hand, if you are lured by the highest rates advertised in the press and published in periodicals such as *The Bank Rate Monitor*, make sure that the bank is insured, preferably by the FDIC. In 1990 hundreds of banks and S&Ls failed in the United States. Even when those failed banks were insured by the federal government, depositors in some cases were not able to obtain their funds for weeks or months.

## WHAT INTEREST RATES CAN YOU EXPECT?

There is no simple answer since interest rates are in a state of constant flux. The following table indicates what may be expected:

| Type of Account | Interest Rate |
|---|---|
| Regular passbook or statement savings | 5.5% |
| NOW and Super NOW | 5–5.5% |
| Short-term time deposit (91 days) | Indexed to most recent 91-day T-bill discount rate |

| Certificates of deposit and money market deposit account | Indexed to 26-week T-bill discount rate, or average of last four T-bill rates, plus 1/4 percent |
| Repurchase agreement | Determined by financial institution |

There are in excess of $300 billion in regular passbook or statement savings accounts. No doubt some of those funds are in small accounts, and depositors are not concerned with the additional funds that could be earned simply by opening other types of accounts within the same institution. High cash balances in low-paying accounts are a gift to a financial institution. It is certainly to your advantage to earn more rather than less interest by switching.

## TAX-FREE SAVINGS

The trick to tax-free savings is to deposit your money in a tax-free fashion whenever possible. This can be accomplished by saving through a tax-deferred account. Then you are only obliged to pay taxes on the funds (original contribution plus accrued interest) when the account is either closed or the money is paid out. At the moment only retirement accounts and educational savings bonds (both federal savings bonds and state educational bonds) have this status, though that may change in the future for other socially approved benefits. There is one other form of tax-free savings: investing in municipal bonds. (These are discussed in Chapter 9.)

If you are employed, your company may offer an income savings plan or salary reduction plan. Indeed, it may even make a matching contribution. While you cannot touch these funds, other than perhaps to borrow against them for a short period, you may determine how they are to be saved: in a savings account, a mutual fund, a fixed-income fund or company common stock.

Employers may also sponsor pension plans to which they make periodic contributions. These are either defined benefit or defined contribution plans and are not subject to taxation until employee retirement. Under the 1986 Tax Reform Act, employed individuals who have pension funds lost their right to contribute to an IRA on a tax-free basis if their income exceeded $50,000 per working couple or $35,000 per individual. (Accounts opened previously, under the old tax code, can still compound on a tax-free basis. Thus they should be maintained and contributed to even though they are no longer a tax-saving device. In other words, the income contributed is now taxed in the year it is received, but the earnings accumulate tax-free until withdrawn.)

If your income does not exceed those figures, you may be able to make partial contributions, but not the maximum $2,000. Some employers may also sponsor 401(k) plans, a type of qualified cash or deferred arrangement, that they administer. Employers may or may not contribute, but employees can stash a portion of their wages or salary into a retirement nest egg. These plans are taxed only upon withdrawal, that is, at retirement.

For the self-employed and professionals, there are Keogh and SEP accounts—all variations of pension plans that allow a portion of earnings to be tax deferred. Under the Keogh, you may contribute up to $30,000 or 25 percent of earnings, whichever is the lesser. Under the SEP plans, employees are limited to $7,979 (1990), but employers have the same limitations as the Keogh.

U.S. savings bonds, whether purchased as part of a payroll savings plan or purchased directly, are not a deduction against income. It is true that they grow to maturity on a tax-free basis, but they are taxable the year they mature.

All these plans allow for direct deductions against income. A custodial agent, one approved by the U.S. Treasury, such as a bank or brokerage house, must maintain the account, but it may be self-directed by the contributor-beneficiary. This puts you in a position to decide how to save most appropriately.

The new tax laws have changed the way children's funds are taxed. Under the old tax code, parents saved money for their children in their children's names, and the earnings on those funds were taxed at the children's low rates. The new tax code allows only for $1,000 of tax-free income for children under 14 years of age and then taxes any additional income at the parents' rates.

After 14, children are taxed at their own rates. While it may sound premature, it is possible to set up an IRA account for a teenager. The first $2,000 of earnings for a summer's hard work can go directly into this tax-free savings account and be left to the magic of compounding. If nothing more was ever added, the $2,000 would be worth $16,812 in 30 years if compounded at 7 percent.

The new tax code left one additional tax-free savings instrument—single premium life insurance. While most insurance policies (except term) build cash value because of the savings components in the policies, purchasers of single premium life insurance can build tax-free savings immediately, since the large premium is the amount of the face value of the policy. A fixed rate of interest for the policy is assigned when it is initiated. It starts to earn tax-free income immediately, while at the same time it provides funds for high-bracket taxpayers at relatively low costs if they wish to borrow their own money without incurring any tax consequence. Single premium life insurance is just another form of whole life insurance, except the total premium is paid up-front. An annuity is similar to this form of life insurance. Annuities also accumulate on a tax-free basis to provide income on a regular basis at a designated age.


## HOW TO CALCULATE INTEREST RATES

As noted above, interest rates are calculated differently, by various financial institutions. Be familiar with simple interest and compound interest formulas to get the best returns on your money.

Simple interest is the sum of principal times rate of interest times time:

$$I = P \times R \times T$$

Thus the simple interest on $1,000 at 6 percent for one year is as follows:

$$\$60 = \$1,000 \times .06 \times 1$$

Compound interest—that is, interest on interest as well as principal—is calculated this way:

$F = P (1 + R)^T$
$F$ is the total future value.
$P$ is the principal.
$R$ is the rate of interest per year.
$T$ is time in years.

Thus the compound interest on $1,000 at 6 percent for five years is as follows:

$\$1,000 (1 + .06)^5$
$\$1,000 (1.06)^5$

$1,000 (1.338)
$F = \$1,338$

Today it is relatively easy to calculate interest rates with calculators and computers. Nevertheless, it is still easier to look at a table. Table 3.1 is an abbreviated table that shows the compounding of a single dollar.

But savings are not a one-time thing. You will presumably be saving consistently for a number of years. Table 3-2 shows the compounding of a single dollar on a regular basis.

To quickly figure how long it will take to double your money, you can use the rule of 72:

$$\frac{72}{\text{Interest rate}} = \text{Years to double}$$

| Interest Rate (%) | Years |
|---|---|
| 5 | 14.40 |
| 5.5 | 13.09 |
| 6 | 12.00 |
| 7 | 10.28 |
| 8 | 9.00 |
| 9 | 8.00 |
| 10 | 7.20 |
| 11 | 6.54 |
| 12 | 6.00 |
| 13 | 5.53 |
| 14 | 5.14 |
| 15 | 4.80 |

Thus, $10,000 at 10 percent annual interest will become $20,000 in 7.2 years.

Pay special attention to bank advertisements on interest rates. They usually show two figures for any time deposit:

**TABLE 3.1**   Interest Rate Table for Daily Compounding
(360-Day Basis Year)

### ANNUAL PERCENTAGE RATE

| 5.00% | 5.25% | 5.50% | 5.75% | 6.00% | 6.50% |
|---|---|---|---|---|---|
| (WHAT A $1 DEPOSIT WILL GROW TO IN THE FUTURE) | | | | | |
| 1.0520 | 1.0547 | 1.0573 | 1.0600 | 1.0627 | 1.0681 |
| 1.1067 | 1.1123 | 1.1180 | 1.1237 | 1.1294 | 1.1409 |
| 1.1642 | 1.1731 | 1.1821 | 1.1911 | 1.2002 | 1.2186 |
| 1.2248 | 1.2373 | 1.2499 | 1.2626 | 1.2755 | 1.3016 |
| 1.2885 | 1.3049 | 1.3215 | 1.3384 | 1.3555 | 1.3903 |
| 1.3555 | 1.3762 | 1.3973 | 1.4187 | 1.4405 | 1.4850 |
| 1.4259 | 1.4515 | 1.4774 | 1.5039 | 1.5308 | 1.5861 |
| 1.5001 | 1.5308 | 1.5622 | 1.5942 | 1.6268 | 1.6941 |
| 1.5781 | 1.6145 | 1.6518 | 1.6899 | 1.7288 | 1.8095 |
| 1.6602 | 1.7028 | 1.7465 | 1.7913 | 1.8373 | 1.9328 |
| 2.1391 | 2.2219 | 2.3080 | 2.3975 | 2.4904 | 2.6871 |
| 2.7561 | 2.8994 | 3.0502 | 3.2087 | 3.3756 | 3.7357 |
| 3.5512 | 3.7834 | 4.0309 | 4.2946 | 4.5755 | 5.1936 |
| 4.5756 | 4.9370 | 5.3270 | 5.7478 | 6.2019 | 7.2204 |

### ANNUAL PERCENTAGE RATE

| 10.50% | 11.00% | 11.50% | 12.00% | 12.50% | 13.00% |
|---|---|---|---|---|---|
| (WHAT A $1 DEPOSIT WILL GROW TO IN THE FUTURE) | | | | | |
| 1.1123 | 1.1180 | 1.1236 | 1.1294 | 1.1351 | 1.1409 |
| 1.2372 | 1.2498 | 1.2626 | 1.2754 | 1.2884 | 1.3016 |
| 1.3762 | 1.3973 | 1.4187 | 1.4404 | 1.4625 | 1.4849 |
| 1.5308 | 1.5621 | 1.5941 | 1.6268 | 1.6601 | 1.6941 |
| 1.7027 | 1.7464 | 1.7912 | 1.8372 | 1.8843 | 1.9327 |
| 1.8939 | 1.9524 | 2.0127 | 2.0748 | 2.1389 | 2.2049 |
| 2.1067 | 2.1827 | 2.2615 | 2.3432 | 2.4278 | 2.5155 |
| 2.3433 | 2.4402 | 2.5412 | 2.6463 | 2.7558 | 2.8698 |
| 2.6064 | 2.7281 | 2.8554 | 2.9886 | 3.1281 | 3.2741 |
| 2.8992 | 3.0499 | 3.2084 | 3.3752 | 3.5507 | 3.7353 |
| 4.9364 | 5.3263 | 5.7470 | 6.2009 | 6.6907 | 7.2191 |
| 8.4053 | 9.3019 | 10.2941 | 11.3922 | 12.6074 | 13.9522 |
| 14.3116 | 16.2447 | 18.4390 | 20.9295 | 23.7564 | 26.9651 |
| 24.3683 | 28.3697 | 33.0281 | 38.4513 | 44.7649 | 52.1150 |

SOURCE: *The Arithmetic of Interest Rates*, Federal Reserve Bank of New York

**TABLE 3.1**   Interest Rate Table for Daily Compounding
(360-Day Basis Year)   (Continued)

### ANNUAL PERCENTAGE RATE

| 7.00% | 7.50% | 8.00% | 8.50% | 9.00% | 9.50% | 10.00% |
|---|---|---|---|---|---|---|
| (WHAT A $1 DEPOSIT WILL GROW TO IN THE FUTURE) | | | | | | |
| 1.0735 | 1.0790 | 1.0845 | 1.0900 | 1.0955 | 1.1011 | 1.1067 |
| 1.1525 | 1.1642 | 1.1761 | 1.1881 | 1.2002 | 1.2124 | 1.2248 |
| 1.2373 | 1.2562 | 1.2755 | 1.2950 | 1.3148 | 1.3350 | 1.3554 |
| 1.3282 | 1.3555 | 1.3832 | 1.4115 | 1.4404 | 1.4699 | 1.5001 |
| 1.4259 | 1.4625 | 1.5001 | 1.5386 | 1.5781 | 1.6186 | 1.6601 |
| 1.5308 | 1.5781 | 1.6268 | 1.6770 | 1.7288 | 1.7822 | 1.8372 |
| 1.6434 | 1.7027 | 1.7642 | 1.8279 | 1.8940 | 1.9624 | 2.0332 |
| 1.7642 | 1.8373 | 1.9133 | 1.9924 | 2.0749 | 2.1607 | 2.2502 |
| 1.8940 | 1.9824 | 2.0749 | 2.1718 | 2.2731 | 2.3792 | 2.4902 |
| 2.0333 | 2.1390 | 2.2502 | 2.3672 | 2.4903 | 2.6197 | 2.7559 |
| 2.8993 | 3.1284 | 3.3755 | 3.6421 | 3.9298 | 4.2402 | 4.5751 |
| 4.1343 | 4.5753 | 5.0634 | 5.6036 | 6.2014 | 6.8629 | 7.5950 |
| 5.8952 | 6.6915 | 7.5955 | 8.6215 | 9.7861 | 11.1080 | 12.6085 |
| 8.4061 | 9.7866 | 11.3937 | 13.2648 | 15.4430 | 17.9790 | 20.9313 |

### ANNUAL PERCENTAGE RATE

| 13.50% | 14.00% | 14.50% | 15.00% | 15.50% | 16.00% | 16.50% |
|---|---|---|---|---|---|---|
| (WHAT A $1 DEPOSIT WILL GROW TO IN THE FUTURE) | | | | | | |
| 1.1467 | 1.1525 | 1.1583 | 1.1642 | 1.1701 | 1.1761 | 1.1821 |
| 1.3148 | 1.3282 | 1.3417 | 1.3554 | 1.3692 | 1.3832 | 1.3973 |
| 1.5076 | 1.5307 | 1.5542 | 1.5780 | 1.6022 | 1.6267 | 1.6516 |
| 1.7287 | 1.7641 | 1.8003 | 1.8371 | 1.8748 | 1.9131 | 1.9523 |
| 1.9823 | 2.0331 | 2.0853 | 2.1388 | 2.1937 | 2.2500 | 2.3077 |
| 2.2730 | 2.3432 | 2.4155 | 2.4901 | 2.5669 | 2.6462 | 2.7279 |
| 2.6063 | 2.7004 | 2.7980 | 2.8990 | 3.0037 | 3.1121 | 3.2245 |
| 2.9886 | 3.1122 | 3.2410 | 3.3751 | 3.5147 | 3.6601 | 3.8115 |
| 3.4269 | 3.5868 | 3.7541 | 3.9293 | 4.1127 | 4.3046 | 4.5054 |
| 3.9294 | 4.1337 | 4.3486 | 4.5746 | 4.8124 | 5.0625 | 5.3256 |
| 7.7892 | 8.4044 | 9.0681 | 9.7843 | 10.5570 | 11.3907 | 12.2902 |
| 15.4404 | 17.0873 | 18.9099 | 20.9269 | 23.1589 | 25.6290 | 28.3625 |
| 30.6072 | 34.7410 | 39.4332 | 44.7590 | 50.8040 | 57.6653 | 65.4531 |
| 60.6719 | 70.6336 | 82.2307 | 95.7318 | 111.4493 | 129.7470 | 151.0484 |

**TABLE 3.2**  Compound Interest on Annual Savings of One Dollar

| Period | 6% | 7% | 8% | 9% | 10% | 11% | 12% | 14% |
|--------|------|------|------|------|------|------|------|------|
| 1 | 1.000 | 1.000 | 1.000 | 1.000 | 1.000 | 1.000 | 1.000 | 1.000 |
| 2 | 2.060 | 2.070 | 2.080 | 2.090 | 2.100 | 2.110 | 2.120 | 2.139 |
| 3 | 3.184 | 3.215 | 3.246 | 3.278 | 3.310 | 3.342 | 3.374 | 3.436 |
| 4 | 4.375 | 4.440 | 4.506 | 4.573 | 4.641 | 4.710 | 4.779 | 4.914 |
| 5 | 5.637 | 5.751 | 5.867 | 5.985 | 6.105 | 6.228 | 6.353 | 6.597 |
| 6 | 6.975 | 7.153 | 7.336 | 7.523 | 7.716 | 7.913 | 8.115 | 8.514 |
| 7 | 8.394 | 8.654 | 8.923 | 9.200 | 9.487 | 9.783 | 10.089 | 10.697 |
| 8 | 9.897 | 10.260 | 10.637 | 11.028 | 11.436 | 11.859 | 12.300 | 13.184 |
| 9 | 11.491 | 11.978 | 12.488 | 13.021 | 13.579 | 14.164 | 14.776 | 16.017 |
| 10 | 13.181 | 13.816 | 14.487 | 15.193 | 15.937 | 16.722 | 17.549 | 19.243 |
| 11 | 14.972 | 15.784 | 16.645 | 17.560 | 18.531 | 19.561 | 20.655 | 22.918 |
| 12 | 16.870 | 17.888 | 18.977 | 20.141 | 21.384 | 22.713 | 24.133 | 27.104 |
| 13 | 18.882 | 20.141 | 21.495 | 22.953 | 24.523 | 26.212 | 28.029 | 31.871 |
| 14 | 21.015 | 22.550 | 24.215 | 26.019 | 27.975 | 30.095 | 32.393 | 37.301 |
| 15 | 23.276 | 25.129 | 27.152 | 29.361 | 31.772 | 34.405 | 37.280 | 43.486 |
| 16 | 25.673 | 27.888 | 30.324 | 33.003 | 35.950 | 39.190 | 42.753 | 50.531 |
| 17 | 28.213 | 30.840 | 33.750 | 36.974 | 40.545 | 44.501 | 48.884 | 58.555 |
| 18 | 30.906 | 33.999 | 37.450 | 41.301 | 45.599 | 50.396 | 55.750 | 67.694 |
| 19 | 33.760 | 37.379 | 41.446 | 46.018 | 51.159 | 56.939 | 63.440 | 78.103 |
| 20 | 36.786 | 40.995 | 45.762 | 51.160 | 57.275 | 64.203 | 72.052 | 89.960 |
| 25 | 54.865 | 63.249 | 73.106 | 84.701 | 98.347 | 114.413 | 133.334 | 179.048 |
| 30 | 79.058 | 94.461 | 113.283 | 136.308 | 164.494 | 199.021 | 241.333 | 349.829 |

(1) the effective annual yield and (2) the annual interest rate. The difference is a function of compounding. The annual interest rate produces a higher effective yield the more frequently the principal is compounded. As a rule, continuous compounding, or daily compounding, is best. But you must also inquire as to when interest is credited—monthly, quarterly or annually.

Finally, ask your financial institution what penalty is involved should you be obliged to invade the time deposit prematurely. Be aware that some banks simply will not allow untimely withdrawals from CDs or time deposits. While your money is never at risk, such conditions can make for awkward situations and the possible loss of earned interest.

# • 4 •

## *How Much Money Do You Have To Invest?*

How much you can afford to invest depends on a number of items: your capital, your earnings, your career, the number of years to your retirement, your responsibilities, your sense about money and so on.

### THE VALUE OF A NET
### WORTH STATEMENT

Before calculating how much to invest, you will find it useful to cast your own personal balance sheet. Unlike an income statement, which measures your cash inflow, outflow and net profit or loss for a given year, a balance sheet is a snapshot in time in that it monetarily freezes your net worth.

Given all the demands on earnings and income from the cradle to the grave, it is important to assess what you have before deciding how it can be best employed. In short, an inventory of assets is a sound first step on the road of financial planning. This inventory is often called a net worth statement since it is a listing of everything you own (assets) against a list of everything you owe (liabilities). The balance—what remains—is your net worth.

Just as no two individuals are likely to have the same net worth, one year is different from the preceding year. The statement only reflects your position at a given moment in time—usually the last day of the calendar year.

The value of the statement is simple: it provides a baseline or benchmark to measure progress or slippage in your net worth. There is another purpose to a net worth statement, one that is not generally appreciated until it becomes useful or necessary to borrow money. A respectable net worth statement can be a potent document in convincing lenders to lend, be they bankers or brothers-in-law.

A thorough net worth statement can also be a pleasant surprise. When all your ducks are lined up, the effect can be overwhelming—many individuals are worth considerably more than they suspected. Not everything can be evaluated with precision, whether it be your home (purchase price, assessed valuation or current market price) or the indeterminate value of a copyright or special collection. Nevertheless, a consistent approximation will serve the main purpose: it will illustrate how your assets are presently divided. That revelation may in turn suggest a better allocation and/or a platform upon which to build a better financial plan.

A simple net worth statement should include a description of the item, its current value and what percentage of the total it represents. Figure 4.1 illustrates a typical net worth statement.

There is nothing necessarily predictive about such an abstract figure as your net worth. A net worth balance sheet does tell you how your assets are currently deployed. It informs you of the magnitude of your debts and how pressing they might be in various circumstances. If you are thinking about investing, a balance sheet will quickly inform you whether your assets exceed your liabilities and if so, by how much.

**FIGURE 4.1**   Sample Net Worth Statement

| *Assets* | *Percent of Total* |
|---|---|
| Cash or equivalents | ____ |
|     Savings account | |
|     Checking account | |
|     Certificates of deposit | |
| Accounts receivable and/or loans | ____ |
| Bonds | ____ |
|     Corporate | |
|     Municipals | |
| Cars, motor vehicles, boats | ____ |
| Life insurance—cash value and/or annuities | ____ |
| Collectibles | ____ |
| Miscellaneous (appliances, equipment, furniture, furs, inventories) | ____ |
| Jewelry | ____ |
| Stocks | ____ |
| Retirement accounts (IRAs, Keoghs, 401(k)/403(b), SEPs) | ____ |
| Company pension plan and/or profit sharing | ____ |
| Refunds | ____ |
| Trusts | ____ |
| Real estate | ____ |
| Home/condo/co-op | ____ |
| Business interest/partnership | ____ |
| Royalties, tax shelters | ____ |
| Other | ____ |
| Total Assets | ==== |

**FIGURE 4.1**   Sample Net Worth Statement  (continued)

| Liabilities | Percent of Total |
|---|---|
| Accounts payable and/or personal loans outstanding | ____ |
| Private obligations | ____ |
| Bank loans | ____ |
| Real estate mortgage | ____ |
| Taxes due | ____ |
| Credit card debt | ____ |
| Other | ____ |

Total Liabilities  _____

Less Total Assets  _____

Net Worth  _____

If you are asset-rich, investing is another way to diversify your holdings. If your liabilities greatly exceed your assets, analyze your cash flow to see if it allows room for investments. Cash flow is almost as important as your net worth statement since it tells whether you can support an investment program.

Any analysis of your net worth is clearly more valuable if you have a number of consecutive years to work with; trends are then more readily apparent. Nevertheless, some observations and rules of thumb may give insight into your balance sheet and provide information as to your status as an investor or potential investor.

It is important to consider a few factors if you never do anything more than structure a sound savings program. There is no ideal model for all situations, but to anyone considering reallocating his or her assets, age and income must be given proper weight.

For example, a 25-year-old who just purchased a home might show that 90 to 95 percent of all his or her assets are invested in a house mortgage. On the other hand, a 65-year-old might show the home (now fully paid) to be only 50 percent of total assets. The 25-year-old might have a negative net worth, or one that is barely positive, while the 65-year-old would have a hefty net worth.

Table 4.1 shows abbreviated examples of assets for three different stages of life.

As noted, there is no ideal net worth statement for any given age, though more is clearly better than less. In examining your own inventory of assets, keep a few simple rules in mind:

• Do not overweigh one asset to the possible detriment of others. It is possible to put too much money into the largest of all family investments—a new home (or a new business, for that matter). Granted the high cost of housing, depleting all other assets for a down payment can be risky. You leave no financial cushion should you be faced with an emergency. Having your eggs in one basket, no matter how sound the basket or how carefully you watch it, can be a costly mistake.

• A corollary to the previous rule is that it is prudent to diversify your assets, as well as your liabilities. As a rule of thumb, no asset should exceed a third of your net worth. While worse-case scenarios rarely come to pass, ask yourself how the total loss of a given asset would affect your life-style. One of the goals of asset allocation is to temper vulnerability.

For the 25-year-old, it is prudent to start a savings plan, consider some form of life insurance and commence a tax-deferred retirement plan. In this case it is not a ques-

**TABLE 4.1**    Sample Assets for Three Stages of Life

| Assets | Age 25 Amount | % | Age 45 Amount | % | Age 65 Amount | % |
|---|---|---|---|---|---|---|
| Cash | $1,000 | 25 | $ 10,000 | 8.3 | $ 20,000 | 3.6 |
| Savings | 1,000 | 25 | 20,000 | 16.6 | 40,000 | 7.1 |
| Securities | 0 | 0 | 10,000 | 8.3 | 50,000 | 8.9 |
| Insurance | 0 | 0 | 25,000 | 20.8 | 100,000 | 17.8 |
| Real Estate | 0 | 0 | 15,000 | 12.5 | 225,000 | 40.1 |
| Pension | 0 | 0 | 30,000 | 25.0 | 100,000 | 17.8 |
| Miscellaneous | 2,000 | 50 | 10,000 | 8.3 | 25,000 | 4.4 |
| Total Assets | $4,000 | | $120,000 | | 560,000 | |

tion of reallocating assets but of starting to contribute to these other asset categories. A 35-year-old who has greater savings, but just as skewed a distribution, should immediately reallocate those savings into other asset categories.

The other factor besides your age to consider is your earnings and your future earnings capability. This is difficult to project unless you have some special knowledge about wage rates, salary scales or professional income—perhaps all you can do is estimate. One approach is to take your current income and increase that amount by 5, 7.5 or 10 percent, or whatever amount seems relevant to your position. The extrapolated figures are likely to be surprising. If you had a salary of $20,000 that increased by 5 percent each year, it would amount to over $32,500 in ten years.

## SOME QUESTIONS TO ASK
## BEFORE INVESTING

*Are Your Assets Diversified?*    Other than your primary home, it is a reasonable precaution not to have more than a third in any single asset and/or account. There have been years when you would not have wanted all your money in shares of IBM, gold bullion, oil drilling partnerships or farmland.

***How Do Your Liabilities Compare to Your Assets?*** If your liabilities equal your assets, you are in imminent danger of insolvency or worse. At the other extreme, no debt may be psychologically satisfying to many people. Modern society, however, requires the use of some credit or deficit financing since few individuals have the wherewithal to pay cash for everything they buy, whether it be a car, a college education or a house.

***Are You in Danger of a Credit Squeeze?*** You may be vulnerable if you have more current liabilities (debt due within a year) than current assets (cash or equivalents)! This "current ratio" is considered one of the most important factors in business analysis and is no less so in personal finance. Try to keep your current or liquid assets twice those of your immediate debts. You will not then be forced to borrow if your earnings or cash flow dries up or to sell off an asset at an unpropitious time.

***How Much Debt Should You Have?*** There is no "right" level of debt. If your interest charges exceed what you earn from a purchased property or investment, you have a negative cash flow. If the property or investment generates more income than the carrying charges, you have a positive cash flow. If you can earn more money on the borrowed money than it costs to service the debt, you are increasing your net worth. As long as your borrowing produces positive results, you can take on more debt.

***Can Net Worth Tell Whether To Invest?*** Yes and no. In addition to understanding your personal balance sheet, you must also consider your annual income. As a rule, you should seriously think about investing when cash and equivalents, plus monies deposited in CDs, savings bonds and other assets, equal your income.

For example, if your total savings exceed one year's earnings, you are ready to consider an investment program. As long as your income stream is secure, building capital assets from personal earnings is an intelligent and far-sighted activity. If, on the other hand, you are in an occupation noted for erratic earnings, you may feel more comfortable with a larger cushion before starting an investment program.

## HOW MUCH CREDIT SHOULD YOU USE?

Once you have drawn up your personal balance sheet, you are in a better position to evaluate the uses of credit. Some people should never use credit or borrowed funds— they worry too much. Other people should never use credit since they don't know how to use it properly. The bankruptcy courts are full of the latter.

Credit, if not abused, can be a great assistance to an investment program. It provides leverage to increase the potential profit of almost any investment vehicle—from gold to options on futures. But it must be controlled and constantly monitored lest it cause negative leverage.

The largest source of credit in most households is the home itself. Since the 1986 Tax Reform Act, home loans have become a popular way to raise additional funds. However, such loans are only tax-deductible on personal income tax returns if the funds are used for home improvements, educational purposes or medical emergencies. There are limits, of course, on what can be borrowed through this type of second mortgage. The formula employed by banks is as follows:

| | |
|---|---:|
| Present market value | $200,000 |
| Maximum lending level | ×   75% |
| | 150,000 |
| Less mortgage balance | − 75,000 |
| Maximum equity loan | $ 75,000 |

This is one way to capitalize on the built-up credit in your home, whether it be your primary or secondary residence. There are two caveats, however, if you plan to use the funds for investment purposes.

- Interest charges are not deductible from home equity loans if the proceeds are used for investment purposes.
- Investment interest charges are deductible only up to the extent of net investment income.

Credit—that is, your ability to borrow—stems from many sources. You might borrow against your financial assets, such as life insurance, trusts, inheritances or royalties. It is somewhat more difficult to borrow against your real assets, such as jewelry and coin collections. One source of credit that many borrowers overlook is the funds that can be borrowed from retirement accounts, pension plans and salary reduction plans. Though borrowing from these sources is more difficult under the present tax code, the lending rates can be quite attractive. What's more, you are not obliged to "qualify" for a loan and do all the paperwork.

Finally, you may be able to borrow against your investments—stocks and bonds—if you have any. Investment paper is an immediate and cheap source of funds. Brokerage houses will lend you funds either to acquire additional investments or to use the funds in some other way. Margin borrowing uses the equity of your investment as a form of collateral.


## SHOULD YOU BORROW?

That decision clearly will depend on a number of factors, some psychological and some financial. Your net worth may be one guidepost: it might be imprudent to borrow more than 25 or 30 percent of your net worth. If you borrow more than that, you may increase your profits at a faster pace, but you also expose yourself to more rapid losses should your investments run into a spell of trouble.

There is another guidepost as well. Banks and other lenders (but not brokers or insurance companies) may also insist on a reasonable income stream—one that will support the debt. For example, mortgage lenders expect that 25 to 30 percent of a family's gross income will go to the mortgage payment, which in turn determines the price of the home the borrower can afford. No reasonable lender will lend more money than can reasonably be carried by the borrower. And a borrower who takes on too much credit does so at his or her peril.

There may be years when saving is impossible for any number of reasons, not to mention the emergencies when rainy days arrive. Interest rates are hard to project beyond a year or two. The further out in time you go, the less likely you will be guaranteed a favorable rate. Nor is it overly advantageous for you to commit to a long maturity at a fixed rate. A sustained period of inflation can make earnings from long-term savings instruments and insurance annuities look pale indeed. The problems are paradoxical and somewhat intractable:

- How do you save for the future at maximum rates without tying yourself into inflexible or fixed yields that may be disadvantageous in a different economic climate?
- How do you save money faster than the rate of inflation?
- How do you guard your savings against levels of taxation that erode their value?

There is no simple, single answer to what is a complicated situation in which you are beset by changing financial conditions and your path is littered with economic banana peels. One reasonable solution is to complement your savings plan with an investment program.

Only through investing can you make a quantum leap from the necessary but sometimes frustrating activity of saving to the rewarding pleasures of accumulating capital gains. But lest you think of the investment world as a one-way ticket to riches, be aware that investing is subject to the frustrations of capital loss, recession, inflation and economic upheaval. In short, there are no free lunches. Nevertheless, with intelligent planning you might eat better now and in the future.

## Y • O • U • R   M • O • V • E

- Cast a net worth statement before undertaking an investment program.
- Keep your current assets at twice the level of your current liabilities.
- List the percentage of assets in each category.
- Consider the proportion of assets with regard to balance. Take steps to reallocate resources if overweight in one area or deficient in another.

- Estimate future earnings. Project a savings forecast for the near, intermediate and long terms.
- Start an investment program when your assets or your savings equal one year of your income.
- Borrow additional funds for investing only if your earnings (or potential profit) will exceed the cost of carrying the debt, that is, the interest for the borrowed funds. Never borrow more than a third of your net worth.

# • 5 •

# *What Are the Goals of Investing?*

Understanding your objectives and your own nature is a large part of successful investing. These are two anchors in a sea of financial variables.

Before investing your first dollar, it helps to know what your time frame is. Are you investing for short-term, medium-term or long-term objectives? If you have previously invested, a glance at your transactions will reveal your tactics, though perhaps not your intentions. Short-term speculations have a way of becoming long-term investments when the market moves the wrong way.

By definition, successful investing is a long-range endeavor. If you expect immediate results and instant gratification, you are by temperament unsuited to long-term investments. The financial markets are but a reflection of the business world and its activities. Change in business conditions, product line and profit margins can be slow. It takes time to turn around an ailing company or to enhance the prospects of a successful one. The perception of change can sometimes be agonizingly slow. Therefore, investing is a waiting game, one in which you will need more patience than money if you are to be successful.

Long-term investing can mean different things to different people, but in the financial world, long-term commitments are those made for at least five years. Middle-range investments are those between one and five years, while short-term commitments start tomorrow and last for a matters of months, a year or two years.

Many investors have great difficulty matching their investments with their objectives. There are two general goals for the investor to pursue: income and growth. These goals are conditioned by such factors as safety, diversification and speculation. While investors' objectives fall into these two categories, there are not only dozens of investment vehicles—common stock, preferred stock, bonds, debentures, pass-through certificates, warrants, futures and so forth—but thousands of companies, municipalities, governments and alternative issuers of negotiable and tradable securities. In brief, investment objectives are few, but the investment world is enormous.

How does one match the investment with the objective? For the moment, it is important to understand what is meant by income and growth. Then it is appropriate to review how the characteristics of safety, diversification and speculation affect the selection of securities.

## INVESTING FOR INCOME

*Income* is the yield (or return) from invested funds. From common or preferred stock, income is derived from the dividend. *Dividends* are that portion of net earnings a company passes on to its shareholders. Corporations usually pay dividends quarterly (four times a year) to stockholders of record as of a specific date.

Income from bonds is called *interest*, a kind of rent payment for the use of the money you lend. Bonds from corporations pay interest twice a year, usually on June 30 and December 31. If bonds are registered, payment will come in the mail to the person whose name appears on the corporation's books. If the instruments are bearer bonds, a coupon must be presented to a bank or brokerage house in order to receive payment.

To make meaningful comparisons, you need to know the current yield rather than just the fixed interest rate. The other type of yield that concerns investors is yield to maturity. Thus the yield to maturity will include the additional $50 that was the difference between the purchase price ($950) and the redeeming or par value ($1,000). The yield to maturity in this case is 8.6 percent if the 8 percent bond had 15 years to maturity.

An investor should ask either the bank or the brokerage house to supply the yield to maturity, or he or she should consult a table of bond values. Since bonds are constantly selling at premiums or discounts, it is imperative to know the yield to maturity in order to evaluate true income.

Bond interest remains fixed throughout the life of a bond, but dividend income from stocks can go up or down. Should a company decide to increase a dividend, that action will certainly increase your income. Indeed, many companies, especially utilities, attempt to do just that. Bond income is more stable and predictable than stock dividend income. Nevertheless, some companies pride themselves on unbroken strings of dividend income. Investors traditionally buy the common stock of utilities and telephone companies when they want interest income.

## INVESTING FOR GROWTH

The other reason for investing—and some would say the chief reason—is appreciation of capital, that is, seeing your money grow. Money in the bank does not appreciate: the bank only promises to pay you (in most types of accounts) what you originally deposited plus the accumulated interest.

Fixed-income investments promise essentially the same thing: to pay back your principal upon the maturity of the debt. Whether monthly or semiannually, the debtor periodically pays interest on the borrowed sum. Rarely does the debtor pay back more than originally promised. It is possible to buy bonds at a discount from par (less than face value) and to sell them at a premium (more than face value). The ability to do this rests largely on timing and interest rate fluctuations. Most individual bond investors do not, however, trade bonds for capital appreciation; they buy them and hold them to maturity.

Therefore, common stock tends to be the main instrument for capital appreciation. Stocks bought specifically for appreciation are called growth stocks.

Growth stock investors are not interested in high dividend payouts. For the investor desiring growth, the smaller the dividend payout, the greater the amount of earnings to be reinvested in the business. This not only causes a stockholder's equity to increase in value but enables the company to maximize its ability to grow. For example, it can then spend more on research and development or increase its sales force.

Regular growth stocks are riskier than blue-chip securities, but they are not as risky as high-growth stocks. Over time blue chips have had a total return—dividends plus capital appreciation—of 7.5 percent a year. The total return for regular growth stocks is 9 to 9.5 percent. High-growth stocks, on average, return something on the order of 11 percent—virtually all of it from capital appreciation. High-growth companies tend to be in start-up ventures and new technology; even if they have earnings, they rarely use them for dividends. A sound growth investment is one in which earnings increase in an appreciable and constant fashion. The profits of such an investment increase in all types of economic weather and into the foreseeable future. Some economists define a growth company as one that grows by at least 10 percent a year, while others think the figure should be closer to 20 percent. In brief, earnings growth is a dynamic process that can be expected to translate into an increase in a stock's market value.

Growth stocks can be found in every industry. Of late some of the more popular growth stocks have been Home Depot, Disney, Wal-Mart, Apple, Microsoft and MCI.

## WHAT IS ADEQUATE DIVERSIFICATION?

It is important to look at how the goals of income and growth are conditioned by techniques to minimize risk. Common sense dictates that in financial matters, it is prudent to spread your risk by diversifying. Whatever your objective, you will be better protected from future events by holding a variety of investments. One famous stock market operator suggested that one approach is to put all your eggs in one basket—and to watch that basket like a hawk. That style of investing is better suited for the trader or speculator. It is not recommended for anyone else because one misstep and you have egg on your face.

Most individual investors unfortunately tend to do just that—they concentrate their portfolio holdings. Over the years surveys indicate two depressing facts: (1) typical portfolios have only two or three securities in them and (2) portfolios with only a few stocks are apt to suffer far greater losses from business risks than portfolios that have 10 to 20 issues.

Poor diversification leaves your portfolio open to company risk. You can reduce company risk by diversifying, as different sequences of the business cycle have different impacts on companies. Auto companies may boom in the early stages of a business cycle, while food companies may not participate until late in the cycle. Thus diversification can lessen the degree of impact from poor earnings; it also protects you from the vagaries of the business cycle.

Is there an ideal number of investments to spread risk sufficiently? No, but economists suggest that a portfolio of 10 to 15 securities will eliminate 90 percent of company risk. The transaction costs to eliminate all company risk would be prohibitive, even if you had sufficient funds. Even a mutual fund investing in a few hundred issues will not provide sufficient diversification if it is a specialized fund. A utility fund will certainly suffer if interest rates go higher, no matter how many utility companies are included in the fund.

Some institutional investors and individuals have concluded that instead of trying to perform better than the general market averages, they will imitate or mimic the averages through index funds. These will not do worse than the market averages since they are the market in microcosm. These index funds are forms of diversification, guaranteeing only average results.

Not only does diversification call for 10 or 15 issues, but the issues should be in varied industries to maximize this hedging technique. Include those industries that are not closely related to each other in the business cycle, in their product lines or in financial, geographic or political terms.

How do you diversify within the business cycle? There are some rule-of-thumb guidelines that suggest which industries to invest in at the various stages of the cycle.

- *In the revival stage*: Consumer durables—home appliances, autos, retail trade, drugs
- *In the expansion stage*: Capital goods—aerospace, building materials, construction, machinery, electronics
- *In the maturation stage*: Materials—chemicals, mining, paper, petroleum, metals
- *In the contraction stage*: Financial—insurance, banking, real estate

- *In the recession stage*: Utilities and services—electricity, gas, telecommunications, transportation

## Time Diversification

Industry diversification must be complemented by time diversification. No one is able to predict interest rate levels one month, one year or five years in the future. When buying fixed-income securities, try to average out your investment by buying some securities at periodic intervals. The same is true for common stock. By buying (or selling) over a long period of time—six months or a year—you may not get the best prices, but then you won't get the worst ones either.

The same is true with dividend reinvestment, stock reinvestment programs and dollar cost averaging plans. By constantly investing fixed sums at regular intervals over a long time, you can minimize the effects of the market's fluctuations. Time diversification is important for successful long-term planning, but it is clearly not for traders who believe in a quick in and a quick out.

One of the rules of survival and success in the securities markets is that no matter how wonderful, how right or how appealing, you don't want 100 percent of anything. Total commitment to one company or industry, or total commitment to one goal or a singular objective, is a position that is likely to leave you unduly exposed to the unexpected. A high-growth company can falter when its chief executive officer unexpectedly resigns, an interest-sensitive income issue can lose value because of higher rates or a retail company bought for long-term appreciation can have a bad Christmas season. There is no end of horror stories to counter the optimism of a bull market. You are best served by participating in a number of industry categories and by purchasing these securities over a period of time.

In brief, diversification is an attempt to deal with the problem of timing. Since few people are adroit enough to maximize their profits by consistently buying at the lowest point and selling at the highest, averaging is a reasonable formula, a trade-off with market realities.

## DOES SPECULATING HAVE A ROLE?

Speculation has achieved some respectability in the last decade or so. Its newly acquired status is due to the fact that bonds—what some fiduciaries considered the only "true" investments—have badly lagged behind inflation in this century. Bonds have indeed returned the total investment to bondholders, plus interest, but the purchasing power of the returned dollars has been anemic. Safety of principal has made bonds the true investment, but if inflation erodes that principal, what good are hollow bonds?

Stocks were traditionally considered speculative since, by definition, they did not promise to return one's investment. It was a matter of luck if they did. "Prudent man" rules established by the courts in the 19th century and legal restrictions on fiduciary investments (those administered by trustees for the benefit of others) relegated common stock to second-class citizenship until recent years.

What has changed the public perception is the simple fact that the returns on speculative instruments—common stock—have far outpaced bond issues. Indeed, stocks have in the long run outpaced inflation as well.

With their newly certified respectability, common stock investments have repaid their investors more amply than bonds, even though safety of principal has remained in doubt. And before long, the distinction between a common stock investment and a common stock speculation has become blurred. Without rigid definitions it is sometimes confusing to determine which is which.

To most observers, a speculation is an investment that takes on high risk for the prospect of a large reward. Today speculation is not universally denounced but is welcomed as a small portion of a portfolio—say, 5 to 10 percent—provided that the investor can tolerate uncertainty. Speculating is not for everyone.

## HOW DO YOU IDENTIFY
## A SPECULATION?

Speculations are identifiable more by what they are not rather than by what they are. A speculative issue usually does not have consistent earnings; it does not typically have a marketable product, but there may be one on the drawing boards. The company issuing the stock or bond does not have much cash or liquid assets.

Speculative issues do represent wonderfully intriguing stories that are almost plausible—flat television tubes, highly efficient solar energy conversion devices, seismic black boxes for locating oil formations or a cure for AIDS. Indeed, there are responsible companies working on all of these ideas, and some may make a great deal of money for those who speculated and backed them. But most of these speculative ventures will fail because they lack the magic, capital and alchemy to turn lead into gold. Investors who wish to participate in a dream should limit their investment to the level at which a total loss will not devastate or decimate their portfolios.

## A MATTER OF SAFETY

If you want safety, examine both common stocks and fixed-income investments. Safety in the financial world is not easy to define since there are so many variables. Most people, however, hold to the definition that a safe investment means no loss of principal.

This strict definition may well rule out most financial instruments (other than bank deposits), since most of them do fluctuate in price in a free market. Therefore, at any given time, stocks or bonds may be selling at prices below where they were purchased. This price depreciation may be only temporary, but to the investor concerned with absolute safety, the morning newspaper will show a loss of funds. It is, of course, just a paper loss until the securities are actually sold. This perception, however, may be unsettling and may conceivably deter you from the investment scene.

On the other hand, if you realize that fluctuations are part and parcel of the investment process and are not necessarily a threat to the safety of your investments, the financial world may offer you potential rewards for tolerating some uncertainty.

If you are investing for income but are concerned with the safety of common stock, consult the grades assigned by the financial service agencies such as Standard & Poor's Corporation. Safe or investment-quality issues are assigned one of the top three rankings: A+, A and A-. In the bond world, safe or investment-quality issues are assigned one of the top four rankings: AAA, AA, A and BBB.

Furthermore, avoid debt issues whose future payments may be in question, such as highly leveraged junk bonds. You should also pass up debt issues whose payment schedules provide for lump-sum rather than regular income distribution since they provide you with no income stream. Securities that fall into that category are U.S. savings bonds, zero coupon bonds and some unit trusts that distribute net investment income (and capital gains) only annually.

Remember, if you are primarily concerned with income and safety, don't reach for the highest-yielding instruments. The highest yield within any given group is a sign of potential trouble. One of the most recent examples of this "yield" madness occurred in the pools of mortgage obligations (pass-through certificates) in 1986 as investors reached for the very highest pools. When interest rates came down, the residential mortgage holders in those pools moved to refinance their home loans. This in turn rather quickly reduced the yields to those pass-through certificates.

In the category of stocks, preferred issues with their fixed dividends as a rule offer more safety than common stock. But as with bonds, it is important to have, at the very least, a BBB rating for the preferred issue.

In the category of common stocks, an investor with income and safety in mind should consider only companies that have a track record of lifting their dividend consistently and rapidly for at least a decade. Rising dividends reflect strong earnings for a company. The shareholder should want to see growth of dividends stay abreast or ahead of increases in the CPI.

If you are primarily interested in growth but are still concerned with safety, the rankings by the financial credit agencies are no less important. Growth companies at times suffer from financial stresses of various kinds: they expand too quickly, they become overindebted, their inventories become excessive or their cash flow declines. The agencies monitor the corporate financials and give an early warning if imbalances are likely to detract from company growth.

Remember, rankings are not a forecast of future market price performance. Rankings are largely an appraisal of past performance, especially of earnings and dividends. Nevertheless, an investor in growth situations will pay special attention to any change in these rankings for the sake of safety.

# • 6 •

## *Which Goals Are Right for You?*

Whether you should emphasize growth or income securities has a great deal to do with your life-style, career, family structure, income, responsibilities both now and in the future and, of course, your age.

In general, capital appreciation should be the goal of investors between 25 and 45 years of age. You need an aggressive investment program early in your working career, after you have sufficient savings. At this stage in life you should continue to implement your savings, but it is appropriate to seek strong growth in the assets available for investing.

After 45, consider adding income to your portfolio. If your previous investment experience has been profitable, you now have a larger base of funds with which to work. You might wish to place 25 percent of your portfolio into either fixed-income bonds or common stock with high dividends.

At 65, or at retirement, reduce your exposure to growth stocks to 25 percent. Some authorities suggest that your whole portfolio be placed in income securities when you retire. Perhaps, but the combination of longer life expectancy and constant inflation argues for a continued commitment to growth stocks. Your assets should always contain some elements of appreciation since you can never be certain about what unexpected expenses you might face.

Moreover, the upward progression of income taxes indicates that postretirement taxation may be far higher than is generally expected. The only way you can hope to offset the erosion of your estate is by continuing to invest a portion of your portfolio in common stock.

It is clear that these scenarios must be modified to suit your personal situations. If you need additional income earlier in life, because of medical conditions or the special educational needs of your children, you will be obliged to reduce your commitment to growth stocks. Or you might opt for further income if your earnings are not advancing as quickly as you hoped. On the other hand, a windfall inheritance, an abundance of fee income or a rapid promotion may all provide additional funds for growth securities.

## WHICH SECURITIES WILL MEET YOUR GOALS?

The universe of securities is vast. There is no end of investments, each with its own special characteristics and purposes. To make things somewhat more confusing, many have overlapping functions; or to put it differently, one security may serve two purposes. Some stocks have both high dividend yield and growth potential, while others have neither one nor the other. Some bonds offer high interest coupons plus the potential for capital appreciation, while others do not.

The following six categories cover a wide range of securities that offer either income or growth. For diversity and safety, it is worthwhile to select a number from each group. For example, an investor seeking income might have 40 percent of his or her portfolio in preferred stock, 20 percent in blue chips and 40 percent in bonds. An investor seeking growth might put 33 percent in common stock, 33 percent in blue chips, 14 percent in speculative issues and 20 percent in money market funds waiting for potential investments. Since there is no perfect or ideal positioning in the securities markets, a directed, delicate balance will provide the best solution to portfolio planning.

|  | Income (%) | Growth (%) |
|---|---|---|
| Common stocks | | 33 |
| Preferred stocks | 40 | |
| Blue-chip stocks | 20 | 33 |
| Speculative issues | | 14 |
| Bonds | 40 | |
| Money market funds | | 20 |

You can attempt to simplify the process by looking at broad categories. In the bond market, bonds tend to sell primarily on yield, a fact reflected in a bond's rating. A bond investor is interested in safety, yield and maturity date. Standard & Poor's and Moody's provide the key to safety, while yield and maturity are obvious.

In the final analysis, most bond investors do not care whether their interest payments come from telephone companies, gas and electric utilities, shipping companies or waterworks systems. If they are primarily concerned with safety, they buy government-guaranteed paper. If they are primarily concerned with tax-free income, they buy municipal bonds. Bond buyers need to keep an eye only on one item—the credit watch list. Should a rating agency substantially change a rating, there is apt to be a strong impact on the price of that issue.

Evaluating common stock is more difficult. *Investor's Business Daily* lists 200 industrial groups with numerous issues in each group. They can be reduced to six basic sectors: (1) capital goods, (2) consumer items, (3) financial services, (4) materials and mining, (5) service industries

**FIGURE 6.1**   Matrix of Two Ways To Look at Common Stock

| Investment Characteristics | Capital Goods | Consumer Items | Financial Services | Materials and Mining | Service Industries | Utilities |
|---|---|---|---|---|---|---|
| **Main Investment Sectors** | | | | | | |
| Investment | | | | | | |
| Blue chip | | | | | | |
| Speculative | | | | | | |
| Growth | | | | | | |
| Blue chip | | | | | | |
| Speculative | | | | | | |
| Cyclical* | | | | | | |
| Defensive* | | | | | | |

*There are blue-chip and speculative issues in each category, but the distinctions are perhaps less clear.

and (6) utilities. Most companies will fall into one of these groups.

Another way of categorizing common stock is by its characteristics, some of which were already discussed:

- *Blue-chip stocks*: Some of America's largest companies as represented by the Dow Jones Industrial Average
- *Income stocks*: High-dividend-paying, largely utilities
- *Cyclical stocks*: Industrial companies whose prices move in tandem with the business cycle
- *Growth stocks*: Businesses experiencing faster than average expansion
- *Defensive stocks*: Recession-resistant companies producing necessary staples
- *Speculative stocks*: New ventures that are untested but offer home-run potential

A matrix of these two ways of looking at common stock will help to diversify a portfolio and fulfill the objectives that an investor has in mind (see Figure 6.1).

It may not be possible to find securities in each category. However, if you buy in each group, you will have a reasonably balanced portfolio. By adjusting your portfolio by weight—more of this and less of that—the objectives of income and growth, conditioned by safety and diversification, may all be met.

## Y • O • U • R    M • O • V • E

- Know what your primary goal is. If you require periodic income, consider the common stock of conservative utilities and telephone companies for dividend income. Also consider securities from the fixed-income market, such as corporate bonds and government issues.
- If you wish to see capital appreciation, growth issues are best suited to your needs. The quality of growth companies is highly diverse. Therefore, make sure you evaluate a corporation and follow the rankings of one of the rating agencies.
- If you seek safety within the context of the stock market, whether investing for income or growth, make sure you select ten or more securities.
- Stock selection is apt to be more successful if done within the time frame of the business cycle. Get a sound fix on the business cycle before making commitments.
- Never put more money into a speculative issue than you can afford to lose. In no event should your portfolio have more than 10 percent of its funds in speculative issues.
- Avoid the fatal error of reaching for the highest yields since this is often a sign of problems rather than generosity.

# • 7 •

## *How Comfortable Are You with Risk?*

Whether you can afford to take chances is a subjective question. Base your answer on a number of factors that will indicate (1) whether you are financially secure enough to take advantage of the investment world and (2) the extent to which you are personally comfortable in dealing with financial risks.

Your financial condition must take into account your net worth, your present earnings, your own and your family's earnings potential, the likelihood of inheritances, the monetary demands made upon you and the needs you feel obliged to fulfill.

Whether you should or should not invest also depends, quite frankly, on how you feel about money. Investing is perceived by many to be overly risky. There should be no delusion on this point. There is some risk in any investment. After all, to invest means "to employ money in the purchase of anything from which interest or profit is expected" (*Oxford English Dictionary*). The operative word here is expected, not guaranteed. A reasoned and intelligent approach can reduce that risk, but it is virtually impossible to eliminate all risk.

Financial risk is naturally viewed differently by individuals, but one's view has much to do with income levels. One Federal Reserve study noted that as income goes up, families become less averse to taking on financial risk.

Households report that, on average, 43 percent would take no financial risks with their investments. That figure is only 17 percent for families earning between $50,000 and $100,000 and 9 percent for those earning between $100,000 and $150,000.

Thus, the phrase "know thyself" is as important today as it was in Delphic times, when the Greeks were admonished to "know" themselves. One's state of mind concerning money has much to do with risk. Risk can be handled in many ways—from total avoidance to total acceptance or from a completely hedged position to a completely exposed position.

## WHAT ARE YOUR COMFORT ZONES?

One way to understand risk is to decide which "risk personality" fits you best. There are three basic types:

1. *Risk-averse individuals.* These are people who, in short, hate to lose. Regardless of how much they win or might win, losing causes far more pain than gain brings pleasure.
2. *Risk-neutral individuals.* They can take or leave risk. Losing doesn't particularly depress them or create anxieties. Gain is pleasurable, but their sense of winning and losing is roughly in equilibrium.
3. *Risk lovers.* These people receive far more satisfaction in winning than they receive pain in losing money. They are prone to gambling.

How do you know if you are being put too much at risk? And is it really a good idea to lower risk? Investing is not a riskless endeavor, nor perhaps should it be. Going back to first principles, reward should be commensurate with risk. The problem for investors is adjusting that level of risk to their own appetites and tolerances.

In the financial world, it was long thought that investors were all risk-averse, that they shied away from situations of chance or situations where there was greater likelihood of deviation from the expected return. This gospel was dramatically undermined with the enormous growth of the market for options and other financial derivatives in the 1970s and 1980s. While such instruments can be used equally for hedging—a technique to reduce risk—many investors were lured to those markets to increase their rate of return.

Contrary to accepted wisdom, many investors were willing to accept higher levels of risk than previously thought. Whether there are other measurable differences in risk personalities is under intense study—(e.g., Are the young more prone to risk than the old? Do men take more chances than women? Are the rich more averse to risk than the poor?).

There are no definitive answers, though the financial community would like to be better able to match risk tolerance with an investor's objectives, especially in this era of liability litigation. One conclusion, arrived at after lengthy study by Professor Frank Farley of the University of Wisconsin, has found that there is a definite Type T, or thrill-seeking personality. This risk lover tends to believe in God more than the meek investor. When theistic investors make an investment mistake, Farley notes that "they bounce back. They have a sense they've got God on their side."

## CHECK YOUR RISK PERSONALITY

Taking the risk test in Figure 7.1 might help you define your tolerance for uncertainty.

**FIGURE 7.1**   Risk Test

---

1. Are you self-employed?

   a. Yes
   b. No

2. How much life insurance do you carry?

   a. None
   b. $10,000
   c. $100,000+

3. How often do you have a physical checkup?

   a. Irregularly
   b. Every five years
   c. Once a year

4. Do you drive without a seat belt?

   a. Yes
   b. No

5. If a new stock investment fell 10 percent shortly after you purchased it, without any change in the company's fundamentals, what would you do?

   a. Sell immediately
   b. Do nothing
   c. Buy more shares

6. What percentage of your total savings are you committing to the stock market?

   a. 90 percent
   b. 10 percent
   c. 50 percent

7. How many times have you changed jobs in the last ten years?

   a. Never
   b. Five times
   c. Two times

8. What would you do if you lost $500 at craps in Las Vegas and were broke?

   a. Try to get even by borrowing from a friend
   b. Leave the table immediately
   c. Write a worthless check for more chips

---

**FIGURE 7.1**  Risk Test  (Continued)

9. After working 15 years at a large corporation, you decide to make a life change. What would you do if you had accrued $50,000 in your pension fund?

   a. Leave it with the company to manage
   b. Take a trip around the world
   c. Invest in your lifetime dream of owning a small business
   d. Withdraw it to invest in the stock market

10. You've heard what you believe to be some confidential information on the golf course about a public company. What would you do if the information were extremely negative?

    a. Rush out to sell short
    b. Pass the information on to a friend who might use it
    c. Ignore the story
    d. Research the situation before acting

11. Your brother-in-law, a real estate agent, is quite certain that a developer is acquiring property for a shopping mall. What would you do if he could get an option on a likely parcel?

    a. Dip into your savings to buy the option
    b. Borrow money on a credit card
    c. Look for a few of partners
    d. Pass

12. What would you prefer to be in?

    a. A CD with a sure 6.5 percent yield
    b. An aggressive mutual fund that has performed poorly since you bought it
    c. A utility stock that seems nailed to the wall

13. What would you do if you bought shares in a high-tech company that rose like Halley's comet?

    a. Use a stop-loss order to protect your profits
    b. Buy more stock every time the company's value increased by 10 percent
    c. Use margin money from the broker to pyramid your holdings
    d. Sell as soon as it hits your goal

**FIGURE 7.1**   Risk Test  (Continued)

14. For what reason would your inherent business sense be most justified?

    a.  You won $50,000 on the game show, Wheel of Fortune
    b.  You hit the daily double at the track for $50,000
    c.  You saw your $25,000 stock portfolio double
    d.  You inherited $50,000

15. What do you say to your high-school child who is thinking about job prospects?

    a.  Advise him or her to consider one of the professions
    b.  Propose a career in the armed services
    c.  Advocate an entrepreneurial life
    d.  Suggest the child follow his or her talent?

*Risk Test Answers*

Your level of risk tolerance will help in determining your investment goals. Total the following points:

 1. a 2, b 1          _____
 2. a 3, b 2, c 1     _____
 3. a 3, b 2, c 1     _____
 4. a 2, b 1          _____
 5. a 1, b 2, c 3     _____
 6. a 3, b 1, c 2     _____
 7. a 1, b 3, c 2     _____
 8. a 2, b 1, c 3     _____
 9. a 1, b 4, c 3, d 2   _____
10. a 4, b 2, c 1, d 3   _____
11. a 4, b 3, c 2, d 1   _____
12. a 1, b 3, c 2     _____
13. a 2, b 3, c 4, d 1   _____
14. a 1, b 4, c 2, d 1   _____
15. a 1, b 2, c 3, d 4   _____
      Total:         _____

**FIGURE 7.1** Risk Test (Continued)

A score between 15 and 20 suggests that you are cautious and conservative. Even somewhat risky investments make you uncomfortable.

A score between 20 and 28 indicates that you might take on some risk, but it should be strictly limited.

A score between 28 and 35 suggests a more aggressive investment approach; you can tolerate a fair amount of uncertainty.

Any score above 35 suggests that you welcome chancy and highly unpredictable investments in the search for greater rewards.

## WHAT CAUSES RISK?

There are three major causes of risk: interest rate risk, company risk and market or system risk.

Interest rate risk is due to fluctuations in the prevailing interest rates, which literally change hourly. The fixed-interest market is particularly sensitive to a number of basic financial changes: Federal Reserve System changes in the discount rate; commercial banks adjustment of prime rates; continuing Treasury auctions of bills, notes and bonds; trade imbalances; currency moves and intervention by foreign-controlled banks. All these actions impact on interest rates, immediately and forcefully.

Company risk stems from the specific fortunes of a corporation. The common stock of a company will react to good news and bad news, analysts estimates of future earnings, strikes, boycotts, takeovers and any other economic events that directly and specifically affect a company.

Market or system risk arises from conditions that affect the whole economy. This risk is nonspecific, since all companies or industries are likely to be touched by events such as a recession, war, budgetary crisis or political upheaval due to an assassination attempt or presidential heart attack. All corporations and government securities are affected, though not necessarily equally.

## HOW DO YOU DEFINE RISK?

What exactly is meant by *risk*? The possibility or chance of loss is a simple but accurate definition of risk. More precisely, risk is the deviation from an expected return on your money. One of the most common characteristics of risk is volatility. All investments harbor some degree of volatility, from the most creditworthy U.S. government-guaranteed bonds (excluding U.S. savings bonds, which do not fluctuate in value as they are a savings vehicle rather than an investment asset) to the most speculative cat-and-dog penny stock. Table 7.1 indicates the range of volatility of some of the major types of investment, compared with the relatively stable performance of savings instruments in the last decade.

Savings instruments are not generally considered risky since they do not deviate from their expected return. On the other hand, investment instruments do deviate from expected returns, and the more they deviate, the riskier they are considered.

## HOW IS RISK MEASURED?

Risk translates into uncertainty as it works its way through investment markets. And uncertainty appears in the guise of volatility as prices of investment instruments bounce around. These price adjustments have been called random (hence the common reference to a "random walk"),

**TABLE 7.1**   Table of Volatility of Investment and
                Savings Instruments

| Investments | Volatility (%) |
|---|---|
| U.S. government bonds | +5.5 – +12 |
| U.S. government bills | +5.25 – +14 |
| High-grade corporate bonds | +6 – +12 |
| Dow Jones Industrial Average | –20 – +25 |
| Over-the-counter stocks (NASDAQ) | –25 – +25 |
| High-yield bonds | +10 – +18 |
| *Savings* | |
| U.S. savings bonds | +6 – +7.5 |
| Certificates of deposit | +6 – +8.5 |
| Passbook/statement savings accounts | +5.5 |
| NOW and Super-NOW checking accounts | +4.5 – +5.5 |
| Money market deposit accounts | +5.5 – +8 |

but it would be wrong to conclude that they are mindless. They are consensus estimates by individuals and institutions attempting to calculate true value. And true value, of course, is a moving target.

The volatility of prices can be measured in one of two ways:

1. Against zero or the investment itself. For example, the stock of General Motors is up (or down) 5 percent from the price at which you bought (or sold) it.
2. Against a market basket index or an average of similar items. The most common market averages are the Dow Jones Industrial Average and the Standard & Poor's 500.

Measuring the fluctuations of a security against itself does give some useful information, such as the normal cyclical variation in a given year. The measurement of risk against a broad market of securities is more useful. How

**FIGURE 7.2**   Volatility of Equity Returns

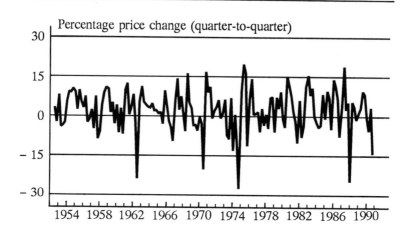

SOURCE: Federal Reserve flow of funds.

does the investment you are interested in stack up against other possibilities?

Modern security analysis has devised a number of criteria to measure risk. (In *The Basics of Stocks*, we will explore this important aspect of investing in detail.) There are literally dozens of important indicators. They range from the price-earnings (P/E) ratio to the number of times the earnings of a company covers its dividends to the amount of cash a company has in the till against its current liabilities.

Financial statistical services give the most prominent rankings for bonds and stocks. Brokerage houses and investment advisory services also rank common stocks. These ratings are based on complex formulas but rest on a company's industry position, product, management, resources and key financial ratios. Earnings and dividends are considered especially important in ranking common stock. Rating agencies assign ranks to common stock similar to the following:

A+    highest
A     high
A–    above average
B+    average
B     below average
B–    lower
C     lowest
D     in reorganization

Another popular measurement of risk is a concept called beta. Through a complicated mathematical formula, all stocks are given a beta rating. This rating system indicates whether the security under consideration fluctuates in line with the market or more or less than the market—the market as measured by Standard & Poor's composite index. A beta rating of 1 indicates that a common stock fluctuates in line with market averages, a rating of 0.5 means that its fluctuations are only half as volatile as the average market and a rating of 1.5 indicates that a common stock's fluctuations are likely to be 50 percent more volatile.

Measuring risk in the bond market has also been done for investors by the rating agencies. Since the reasons for bond fluctuations are considerably different from the reasons why the prices of common stocks bounce around, beta ratings are not used. Bonds move largely in response to interest rate conditions as well as the underlying strength of a corporation and industry. Bonds are, of course, debt instruments. Rating agencies, such as Standard & Poor's, Moody's and Duff & Phelps, rate the value of corporate promises to repay debt and pay interest on that debt when due. (Rating of bonds will be discussed in detail in *The Basics of Bonds*.) Here is an interpretation of rating systems, such as Standard & Poor's, that grade the strength and value of corporate indebtedness:

| Rating | Meaning |
|--------|---------|
| AAA | Highest grade |
| AA | High grade |
| A | Upper medium—sound |
| BBB | Medium—some uncertainty |
| BB | Speculative |
| B | Speculative |
| CCC | Speculative—default imminent |
| CC | Speculative—default imminent |
| C | Speculative—default imminent |
| D | In default—no value |

It is clear that much work has been done to measure risk. In addition to grades from the credit rating agencies, the financial dailies, magazines, newsletters and computer data banks all offer their own interpretations, evaluations and recommendations.

## HOW SHOULD YOUR RISK PROFILE AFFECT YOUR INVESTMENT STRATEGY?

If you are totally risk-averse, stay away from the investment world. Watching your funds fluctuate daily in value will only cause you anxiety. Savings accounts and savings techniques will help you safely obtain the highest yields on your savings.

If you are risk-neutral, the investment world should pose no great problem for you. The limited volatility of the securities markets is but a reflection of differing opinions of what securities are worth. For the most part, such volatility is tolerable to risk-neutral investors. On rare occasions, such as on October 19, 1987, the market's volatility is extraordinary. However, that kind of fluctuation seems to happen once in a decade. Investors who rode out the storm emerged relatively unscathed.

Therefore, risk-neutral investors—whether oriented for investment income or capital growth—have a wide variety of investment vehicles to choose from that will provide safety and diversification. If you have a risk-neutral temperament, stay away from speculative instruments, such as commodity contracts or securities that do not have investment-grade qualities. These instruments are too volatile for risk-neutral investors.

Risk lovers can range over the whole investment world since neither the volatility of such instruments as futures contracts nor the questionable quality of some issues is a deterrent. If you are a risk lover, you welcome the volatility inherent in such instruments since the fluctuations provide not only psychic pleasure but the potential for great profits.

Everyone's risk tolerances are different, but Table 7.2 suggests some possible investment strategies.

No matter what you do in the investment world, there are few guarantees—just different levels of risk. Guarantees do exist in the world of savings. Banks ensure that up to $100,000 in savings and checking accounts will be guaranteed by the federal government. These are, of course, ultimate guarantees since they are backed by the full faith and credit of the U.S. government. In a worst-case scenario, the federal government can always print more money, even if the intrinsic value of those dollars is far different than the original deposits.

Guarantees in the investment world are limited to bills, notes and bonds of the U.S. Treasury. Other guarantees, such as those issued by municipalities on their bonds or by insurance companies on the repayment of principal and interest, are clearly subsidiary to federal guarantees. And that difference in risk is built into the price structure of these investment instruments. The point to remember here

**TABLE 7.2**  Possible Investment Strategies

| Category | Risk-Averse | Risk-Neutral | Risk Lover |
|---|---|---|---|
| Savings | 25% | 20% | 5% |
| Money market/T-bills | 10 | 5 | 5 |
| T-bonds | 25 | 20 | |
| Ginnie Mae | 20 | | |
| Mutual funds | | 15 | 30 |
| Common stock | | 15 | 30 |
| Corporate bonds/preferred stock | | 15 | |
| Municipal bonds | 20 | | |
| Options | | 10 | 15 |
| Futures | | | 15 |

is that there is a difference in guarantees, and the marketplace compensates for that difference.

Investors and speculators have a vast department store in which to shop—from the $4 trillion government securities market to the rarely traded securities on some foreign bourses. And in between, there are 2,500 companies listed on the New York Stock Exchange, 1500 on the American Stock Exchange and some 40,000 traded in the over-the-counter (OTC) markets. The menu is virtually endless, and your choices are limited only by your effort and imagination in the decision-making process.

Bear in mind that the financial world is constantly changing and will continue to do so. New products are created almost daily, and not all of them are successful. Some instruments in the following groups, such as exchange traded options or collateralized mortgage obligations, hardly existed a decade or so ago. Now they seem to have been always with us. Other new products, such as certain commodity contracts, were trial balloons and have vanished without a trace. A prudent investor will wait until a new product—whether a complex financial instrument or the common stock of a new corporation—has proved itself in the marketplace.

There are, quite simply, two types of investments you should steel yourself against: (1) the new product that solves all financial conundrums and (2) the new stock, closed-end fund or municipal bond of which they are offering you the last share or piece, since the offer is destined never to be repeated at this price. Financial instruments are not like elastic socks—one item does not fit all needs. Moreover, the investment world is replete with products, and there has never been a shortage of stocks, bonds, options or other instruments.

## Y·O·U·R   M·O·V·E

- Realize that investing entails some risk, no matter how conservative your investment approach. Risk can be hedged but not completely eliminated.
- Attempt to measure your risk tolerance. If putting your money at risk makes you ill, nervous, uncertain or unhappy, then divorce yourself from the investment world. Your choice is either not to participate or to let a professional money manager handle your investment affairs.
- If you can withstand daily price fluctuations and normal market volatility, a balanced investment program may increase the rate of return on your funds, compared to straight savings.

# • 8 •

## *Investing in Stocks*

### THE PROS AND CONS

The advantages of long-term investing remain undeniable. No other investment vehicles have performed so spectacularly in the bull market of the 1980s as have common stocks. Equities have consistently outperformed fixed-return investments over longer periods. One study conducted by T. Rowe Price shows that if you put $2,000 a year into equities for 20 years at the year's stock market peak (the worst time for investing) and reinvested the dividends quarterly, you would have had an overall current-dollar return of $177,772 by January 1, 1990. In brief, the stock market has done extraordinarily well for the long-term investor and is likely to continue to do so throughout the 1990s.

The disadvantages rest, to a large degree, in timing and short-term trading. There are, of course, any number of weak companies to invest in, and they consequently show poor investment performance. If you select inappropriate companies, the results are likely to be dismal and you will lose capital.

But perhaps the real disadvantages in the market are poor timing and lack of patience. Many investors act like traders, though they have neither the talent nor the information for that professional occupation. Timing is always difficult, but it is almost impossible if you turn over your portfolio constantly. Your investments never have time to appreciate, and the commission costs eat up whatever meager profit you might make in the short term. Investment success is a waiting game; if you are temperamentally unsuited, you should either not invest or should perhaps concentrate your energies in speculating.

## COMMON STOCK

### What Is It?

The most popular vehicle in the investment world is common stock. Representing a fractional portion of ownership in a company, common stock or shares give the owners the right to participate in a company's profits. Stockholders or shareowners also have the right (except with some special classes of stock) to elect a board of directors, which in turn hires the company's managers. Shareholder democracy generally consists of one share– one vote to be exercised at the annual meeting.

### How Safe Is Stock?

As owners, stockholders assume all the risks of ownership. When business goes well, a company can pay a dividend, and the price of shares will appreciate. Conversely, when business is slack, a company will reduce or eliminate the dividend, and the price of the stock will depreciate. Thus, there are market risks in owning a company's stock––risks that are largely absent if you only lend a company money by purchasing its bonds (unless, of course, poor business forces the company to suspend bond payments). In large and/or well-managed companies, risks are reduced because of diversification, better management, superior marketing, a special product rather than a commodity and other positive business attributes. Nevertheless, the equity owner is subject to the vicissitudes of business—-but then no pain, no gain.

## Where Are Stocks Sold?

Stocks can be bought directly from a company in some instances or, in the case of an initial public offering, from a brokerage or investment banking house. These purchases in the primary market are relatively rare. It is far more common to buy and sell stock in the secondary market. In the United States there are seven stock markets-—New York, American, Midwest, Pacific, Philadelphia, Boston and Cincinnati, plus the over-the-counter (OTC) markets (essentially a network of traders and broker-dealers that transact business via telephone and television monitors).

Securities sold on the exchanges are listed—that is, they meet the specific requirements of the exchanges on which they are traded. The purpose of the listing requirements is to ascertain that there is public interest in a company, there is a history of profitability, the firm has sufficient capital to carry on as a public company and the company already has a sizable core of public stockholders. Shares traded in the OTC markets, especially on the National Association of Securities Dealers Automated Quotations (NASDAQ) system also must meet some requirements, but these are structured to fit small and fledgling companies.

## What Does It Cost To Buy and Sell Stock?

Initial public offerings are usually sold on a net basis—that is, the customer pays no brokerage commission when the shares are purchased from an original underwriter. Of course, most shares are bought in the secondary market, from previous shareholders. These shares are subject to the fixed commission schedule of the brokerage house with which the customer is dealing. Full-service brokers charge higher commissions than discount brokers, but they offer advice plus other services not provided by discount brokers. A full-service broker might charge as much as a 1 or 2 percent commission fee, while a discount broker charges half or less that of a full-service broker's commission. Commission charges, however, can be negotiated downward for larger or more active accounts, especially with full-service brokers.

Shares purchased in the OTC market are marked up to allow for a market-maker's profit, sometimes as much as 5 percent. With the computerized central trading system through NASDAQ, customers are assured of getting the best publicly quoted price in this negotiated market. In general, buying and selling listed common stock in relatively modest 100-share amounts, or round lots, can carry a commission charge of 1 to 2 percent. In the OTC market you may pay a net price, as the dealer's profit is included in the price.

## How Liquid Is the Market?

Owners of common stock can enter and exit the market at will. The stock exchanges run continuous markets, as do the OTC markets, and they rarely run out of products to sell or buyers to buy. The exchanges maintain auction markets with designated auctioneers or specialists. As exchange members, it is the function of these specialists to maintain a fair and orderly market in a given stock, as well as to step in if no seller or buyer is present and no comparable orders are on the specialist's book of open orders. (The specialist maintains a book or listing of price orders that are away from the market, that is, they are not exercisable at the current market price. When the market price reaches the levels of the orders on the book, they then become market orders and are executed.)

In the OTC market, there is no one specialist, but the half-dozen or dozen market makers make it a virtual certainty that there will always be someone to sell or buy stock. Understandably, the more exotic the security is, the fewer the participants. Markets are clearing mechanisms—which is another way of saying that at some price level almost everything can be sold or bought.

## How Much Can You Make?

There is no easy answer to this question. As previously indicated, there are historical averages that indicate the long-term return on equity investments is on the order of 9 percent. In bull markets, participants do better, and in bear markets, they do worse. How well you do is a function of the following factors:

- How much work you do in analysis
- How useful your information is
- How solid your judgments are
- How emotional you are in your behavior

Buying stock allows for unlimited appreciation on the upside. But you can also make money on the other side of the market by selling overvalued stock. Selling stock short (that is, selling shares that you borrow from a broker with the intention of buying an equal number of shares later at a lower price to replace the original shares) is limited by a floor of zero since a security can only become worthless. Few people sell securities short, but it is a perfectly legitimate way of profiting in equities.

## PREFERRED STOCK

### What Goal Does It Satisfy?

Preferred stock provides more security than common stock. It is an issue that provides a relatively high dividend return, one that is fixed for the life of the issue. The holder of preferred stock will not experience the full benefits of corporate success as reflected in higher common stock prices, but the holder will certainly have a set and secure return on invested funds.

### What Is It?

Common stock represents the last claims on a company's assets; that is, the owners get paid after all other creditors have had their claims attended to in a bankruptcy or liquidation. As owners, they sit on the bottom of the totem pole. This position can be altered somewhat by owning preferred stock in a company. Preferred stockholders are legal owners, but they should consider themselves claimholders, as do bondholders. Not all companies issue preferred stock, but those that do, offer shareowners a veritable combination plate. If a company prospers, the value of the preferred shares will appreciate, though not as much as the common stock; if a company fails to prosper, the value of the preferred shares will contract, but not to the extent of the fall in price of the common stock.

Preferred stock is usually issued to offer buyers the best of both worlds. It represents a form of senior ownership, while it also offers a fixed dividend, as does a bond. This hybrid nature of preferred shares makes them a safer investment than common stock.

### How Safe Is It?

While preferred stock appears to be safer than common stock, there are some drawbacks. Preferred stock will not participate in any increase in the rate of dividends, nor will it enjoy any stock splits or the benefits of a company's recapitalization. And the price of preferred issues rests to a large degree on prevailing interest rates. If rates rise, the value of the shares is likely to be adversely affected since they sell mainly on their yields (the rate of return on the investment).

Nevertheless, purchasers of preferred issues are more concerned with steady income than maximizing their returns by chasing interest rates. The fixed dividend provides a cushion of safety. If a company improves its fortunes, preferred owners stand to benefit, though more modestly than owners of common shares.

### Where Are Preferred Issues Traded?

As with common stock, preferred issues are traded on the exchanges as well as on the OTC. Commission costs are also comparable. However, in general there are fewer shares available for preferred issues since they are especially attractive to other corporations, as much of that dividend income can be received tax-free. Thus, the issues you are interested in may not be readily available at all times, or they may be priced at levels that produce unattractive dividend yields on an aftertax basis.

## How Much Can You Make?

Preferred issues are not as volatile as a company's common stock, but they rise and fall in a more stately fashion. There are two subspecies of preferred issues that offer additional ways of profiting from the fortunes of a business: (1) cumulative preferred issues and (2) convertible preferred issues. Cumulative preferred issues accumulate their dividends in the years that a company is, for whatever reason, unable to pay dividends. Therefore, holders of the cumulative preferred will be paid all the owed dividends before the common stockholders see a penny of dividend income. Convertible preferred issues can, at some fixed ratio, be turned into common stock. Holders of the convertible preferred are paid their fixed dividend, but they may also exchange them for common stock if a company is quite successful. This call on the common stock makes the convertible preferred desirable but also somewhat more volatile than the plain preferred issue.

# • 9 •

## Investing in Bonds

### WHAT ARE THE ADVANTAGES?

When considering the investment world, every investor, potential investor and saver should investigate the bond market. Quite simply, bonds are government or corporate IOUs, promises to pay back the original borrowed principal at a fixed date in the future. For the use of borrowed funds, the borrower will pay the lender a fixed rate of interest, usually semiannually, known as the coupon rate. Bonds are called debt securities or fixed-income issues as they guarantee repayment and a steady stream of interest payments.

There are two major considerations for individuals thinking about debt securities: (1) high income and (2) safety. A widely held assumption in the investment world states that it is better to be owed money than to own assets. In other words, it is more secure for individuals to receive regular and steady payments from the governments and major corporations to whom they have lent money than to be owners of all but the most prime corporations.

The price of owned assets may go up, down or remain rather fixed for long periods of time. By buying debt—that is, the bond issues of governments, agencies or the largest, most resourceful public corporations—one can be reasonably assured of a steady income flow—and a predictable return on assets. The stock markets have a good deal of past price action on which to predict the future, but it is obviously hard to predict with certainty where stock prices will be 12 months or 5 years from now. Many people feel the bond market is more predictable and safer.

This steady flow of income from bonds is quite desirable for many investors, and probably every portfolio should have some investments that throw off regular yields. (The prices of bonds may fluctuate, but the coupon rate will remain the same for the life of a bond.) Indeed, some investors should have nothing but fixed-income assets in their portfolios (e.g., single retired individuals who need all the income they can muster to maintain their income streams).

The other element—safety—arises from the fact that bonds are considered senior securities, that is, obligations companies pay almost regardless of business conditions. Government bonds—whether issued by the U.S. government, foreign governments or state and local authorities— all have some form of taxing or revenue-raising ability. Bonds have historically been considered a safer investment than common stock. It is extremely rare for a quality bond issue to default, though that action is not unknown.

## ARE THERE ANY DISADVANTAGES?

Bonds, whether private or public, do have a downside. As debt instruments, they earn no profits, no matter how successful the company that issued them. At maturity bonds promise only to pay face value plus the coupon or stated interest rate.

While the United States has never defaulted on its bonds, other sovereign states have been known to do just that when their forms of government abruptly change.

Very high-yielding corporate bonds (commonly known as junk bonds because of their low credit ratings) were severely tested in 1990, and many issues defaulted. Still other junk issues saw their prices cut in half when Drexel Burnham Lambert (the issuer of many junk bonds) went bankrupt. Junk bonds are creatures of the 1980s and suffered in the business recession of 1990–91. It would not be unreasonable to expect some problems among companies issuing such paper since they are highly indebted and could have trouble servicing their obligations when business is poor and credit tight.

Interest rate risk is very much part and parcel of the bond market. When interest rates rise, bond prices fall, and vice versa. If prevailing interest rates move up, all fixed-interest investments react by moving down. And the reverse is also true: when interest rates go down, bond prices appreciate. This inverse ratio is confusing to some investors, but it is a simple reflection of the facts of life. Why should anyone buy an old bond issued with a low yield when new bonds (reflecting today's interest rates) are paying higher yields? To be competitive, the old bond must fall in price so that the old coupon is equal to the higher yields. For example, if the interest rate on a newly issued bond is 9 percent, an old $1,000 bond with a 10 percent coupon rate will rise to $1,111 (1,000 ÷ 9) but will also fall to $909 if interest rates move to 11 percent. In short, old bond issues must constantly adjust their prices to reflect current interest rate levels.

A number of other factors also determine a bond's price (e.g., supply and demand and years to maturity). A long-term rise in interest rates, such as the one that took place at the end of the 1970s, can send the price of medium-term and long-term bonds down fast. Conversely, the fall in interest rates from 1982–86 caused a major bull market in bonds.

Finally, in a period of inflation, long-term debt instruments are dubious holdings. While they return at maturity the number of dollars originally promised, they do not return purchasing power. This loss of purchasing power is one of the chief arguments against total reliance on a portfolio of bonds. There is a trade-off between bonds and stocks: they complement each other in well-balanced portfolios. You must decide what is the right equilibrium for your holdings at any given stage of life.

## WHAT FIXED-INCOME INVESTMENTS ARE AVAILABLE?

As noted previously, there is a staggering variety of fixed-income investments, ranging from U.S. savings bonds to mortgage obligations and from zero coupon bonds to revenue bonds. How do you sort them out, and how do you know which are appropriate for your needs?

The following discussion of fixed-income investments will highlight their reasons for existing, their stability or riskiness of principal and their fluctuations in yield or current income.

## TREASURY ISSUES

### What Are They?

To finance the federal government, the U.S. Treasury issues a variety of bills, notes and bonds. These are sold to the public through a constant series of auctions. The federal government guarantees their redemption when they reach maturity.


## How Safe Are They?

With the full faith and credit of the U.S. government behind them, Treasury issues constitute what many consider the safest investment in the world. Whether you buy short-term (three-month, six-month or one-year) Treasury bills, medium-term (one-year to ten-year) notes or long-term bonds, you are virtually certain to receive your principal back. Though Congress occasionally plays out a prescribed minuet of not extending the debt ceiling, which in turn holds up Treasury auctions and threatens default on loan payments, the U.S. government has paid its debt on time for over 200 years. Treasury paper is considered so riskless that the rating agencies (such as Standard & Poor's and Moody's) do not bother to grade government issues.

Nevertheless, not all government paper is equal in the eyes of the market. Some issues trade at distinctively different yields, even though they all have a call on the government in the final analysis. Treasury paper is, quite simply, issued by the Treasury. The U.S. government also sponsors government agency and quasi-government debt securities. These agency obligations are more enticing because they offer a fractionally higher yield than Treasury paper. The higher yield is to compensate for the assumption that such issues are not quite as safe as Treasury paper, nor quite as liquid or marketable. That is certainly true, but it would be wrong to believe that agency debt has nothing more than a moral obligation of the government behind it. The various agencies were created by congressional acts, and the Congress authorized them to issue securities. Even though these issues do not have a full faith and credit clause to back them, there is virtually no reason to expect that they would not be redeemed should that be necessary.

A few of the more popular agencies are as follows:

- Federal Home Loan Bank Board
- Federal Home Loan Mortgage Corporation (often called Freddie Mac)
- Federal National Mortgage Association (often called Fannie Mae)
- Government National Mortgage Association (often called Ginnie Mae)
- Student Loan Marketing Association (often called Sallie Mae)
- Tennessee Valley Authority
- U.S. Postal Service

Whether the government guarantee is implicit or explicit, these agencies all produce revenues of their own (some are even capitalized with common stock that you may buy) to service their debts rather than rely on the Treasury.

### What Do They Typically Cost?

Treasury bills are sold to the public at a discount from face value. That discount is the basis for calculating the yield that bills pay. For instance, a one-year Treasury bill of $10,000 might sell in the auction for $9,000. One year later the government returns to the winning bidder $10,000, a yield of ($1,000 ÷ $9,000) 11.11 percent. Consequently, the buyer of Treasury bills knows very closely what the yield will be before the auction due to commentary in the financial press and prevailing rates.

Treasury bonds and notes (in denominations of $5,000 and $1,000) are not sold at a discount to reflect their yield but are priced at or near their face value with a fixed rate of interest that will be paid twice yearly. The same is true of agency paper—it pays interest twice a year.

### Where Are They Sold?

Treasury issues can be bought directly from a Federal Reserve Bank at approximately full face value with no commission, or from banks and brokerage houses for the same price but with a nominal commission. New agency paper must be bought from the issuing investment banking syndicate—without any commission fee.

### How Liquid Is the Market?

Since the Treasury market is the largest market in the world, there is instant liquidity. You can enter or exit the Treasury market at any time.

### How Much Can You Make?

Long-term investors who buy original note and bond issues can only make the coupon yield, the interest that the issue is designated to pay. Traders, on the other hand, can buy issues when they are depressed because of high current interest rates, and they can sell them when rates come down. This provides a capital gain, but it is not recommended for long-term investors.

## MORTGAGE-BACKED SECURITIES

### What Are They?

Mortgage-backed securities are certificates covering pools of conventional mortgages. They are issued by private institutions as well as by the federal government. Some agencies, especially the Government National Mortgage Association (GNMA), Federal National Mortgage Association (FNMA) and Student Loan Marketing Association (SLMA), sell mortgage-backed securities. These are a form of pass-through securities—they pass on to investors the interest and principal paid by the original mortgage holders. GNMA, for example, buys a pool of residential mortgages from a mortgage banker, usually in multiples of $1 million. The pool is divided up into certificates of $25,000, which can be purchased by investors.

### What Goals Do They Satisfy?

For their money, investors get a portion of the pool paid out to them on a monthly basis. Thanks to GNMA, mortgage bankers receive cash for their residential mortgages, thus allowing them to make new mortgage commitments. For the investor, these certificates pay interest and a return of principal monthly. They therefore provide a steady cash flow for income-oriented investors.

### How Safe Are They?

GNMA guarantees the pools—the mortgages are usually guaranteed by the VA or FHA. In the private sector, they are insured by mortgage bankers. Thus, a $25,000 pass-through certificate is guaranteed in that it will be paid off. What is not guaranteed is the rate of interest.

### What Do They Typically Cost?

Mortgage-backed securities are sold in denominations of $25,000. It is possible to buy a "used" certificate, one that was issued some years earlier, for a comparably lower price.

### Where Are They Sold?

New issues must be bought from an underwriter or from members of his or her syndicate. Your broker will find a long list of mortgage-backed securities for sale in the secondary markets. To give you an idea of the approximate price and yield in the daily market, typical certificates are listed in the fixed-income area of the business section of your daily newspaper.

### What Does It Cost To Buy and Sell Them?

There is a nominal brokerage charge for the purchase of certificates. The broker-dealer will frequently offer a net price; the commission is part of the final price. In either event, the charge for buying or selling is low.

### How Liquid Is the Market?

GNMA certificates have traditionally been the highest-yielding government-secured paper. But glitches can some-times arise—for example, the rapid fall of interest rates in

1985–86. People owning mortgages taken out earlier—when they were obliged to pay, perhaps 14 or 15 percent—found that it was possible to refinance at 10 or 11 percent. Many did, and the pools suffered a faster payback than originally anticipated. Some pools had "very high speeds" (which refers to the rapid rate at which they were repaid), and the yields in turn were lowered for a while. The lesson here is that you should not reach for the highest-yielding pools, those hyped in advertisements, because they are the ones to first feel the refinancing frenzy.

These pass-through certificates are extremely popular and may even be traded and bought when they are half paid down. The average life is about 12 years for most pools. Thus, it is possible to buy a certificate with six years remaining for about half the original price, depending on interest rate levels. Naturally, the certificate's price will fluctuate, as will all fixed-interest instruments. Another danger, sometimes unappreciated by buyers, is that the monthly check contains both principal and interest. Unless the principal is reinvested, it is possible to spend the principal without knowing it. Finally, it should be clear that while the repayment of principal is guaranteed, the interest payment will vary somewhat. This unpredictable return may be a cause of concern for investors who count on every dollar. Since there is a large market for these certificates, the market is very liquid—you can buy and sell them at any time.

## How Much Can You Make?

Long-term investors will know the exact rate of interest that these issues pay since it is stated upon purchase. However, because of the nature of refinancing mortgages, there is no guarantee that the rate of interest initially stated will last the life of the certificate. If a number of mortgages in the pool are refinanced at lower rates, there may be some fall in the rate of interest paid in subsequent years.

## ZERO COUPON BONDS

### What Are They?

Another new financial instrument—zero coupon bonds (or zeros)—was created in the 1980s and has become very popular with investors who look for fixed and predictable returns on their funds. These are issued by the Treasury and by some corporations and are called strips, since the interest coupons have been removed. They pay no interest but are initially sold at a great discount from their face value. The price at which they are sold reflects the rate of interest at which the bond's price will grow every year. Thus, it is possible to know exactly the yield for the life of the bond when it is purchased.

### What Goals Do They Satisfy?

Zeros have been sought out as near-perfect holdings for retirement accounts and for building nest-egg funds for college education. The certificates or receipts are issued at a deep discount from their face value; the discount depends on the underlying rate of interest on the bonds as well as the maturity date. These new coupon bonds, as the name implies, pay no semiannual interest. There are now issues for virtually every maturity for the next 30 years. Therefore, it is possible to plan ahead in calculating retirement funds or college tuition.

## How Safe Are They?

Since the Treasury strips are issues of the United States, they have the full faith and credit pledge of the federal government. The zero receipts issued by investment banking houses are equally safe since the trust or bank that issues the receipts has Treasury bonds as collateral.

## What Do They Typically Cost?

The U.S. Treasury issues stripped securities (as do some investment banking houses that issue trust certificates representing the underlying Treasury bonds) at very low prices. For example, a ten-year zero strip might be issued for $377 per $1,000 bond. In brief, the zero will appreciate almost 2.7 times by its maturity date (see table that follows). At that level, the zero has locked in a 10 percent rate of interest for the life of the instrument. Each year the zero becomes more valuable until at the end of the tenth year, when it is worth its full face value.

*Zero Value—10 Percent*

| | |
|---|---|
| Year 1 | $   377 |
| 2 | 416 |
| 3 | 458 |
| 4 | 505 |
| 5 | 557 |
| 6 | 664 |
| 7 | 677 |
| 8 | 746 |
| 9 | 823 |
| 10 | 907 |
| Maturity | $1,000 |

## Where Are They Sold?

New issues are sold either by the Treasury or by the investment banking house that has fabricated the receipts. In the secondary market, zero coupon bonds are part of the Treasury market.

## What Does It Cost To Buy and Sell Them?

The commission charges for zero coupon bonds are nominal. They are frequently sold on a net basis, that is, the broker-dealer's commission is included in the price.

## How Liquid Is the Market?

As part of the Treasury market, zero coupon bonds can be sold and bought at a moment's notice.

## How Much Can You Make?

The purpose of zero coupon bonds is to lock in a favorable rate of interest for a long period. Long-term investors know exactly what yield they will earn when the bonds are purchased.

The beauty of zero coupon bonds is twofold. Once a zero is purchased, the interest rate is locked in for the life of the bond. Moreover, they can be bought in denominations as small as $100. The other benefit is that the investor need not buy them in denominations of $5,000 or $10,000 as is the case with Treasury notes and bonds sold through brokerage houses. One can, so to speak, nibble at them, a few now, a few later—all the while taking advantage of their compounding.

Locking in a yield to maturity resolves the problem that plagues typical fixed-interest investments, that is, what to do with the monthly, quarterly or semiannual payments. Thus zeros are eminently predictable. They come as close to a one-decision investment as is possible. Zeros do have a large secondary market and thus can be easily sold, but be aware that they are more volatile than ordinary Treasury or corporate bonds because of the lack of periodic interest payments.

Finally, buyers of zero coupon bonds know exactly what the value of their investment is at any given time, and how much the bonds are yielding. While taxes are deferred in IRA, Keogh and other tax-advantaged accounts, zeros do have a rate of interest imputed to them and so are taxed by the IRS in ordinary accounts.

## MUNICIPAL BONDS

### What Are They?

The "muni" market is a large, disparate emporium of bonds issued by local city, county and state governments, as well as by regional authorities, thruways, turnpikes, ports, terminals, airports and waste facilities. They are all generally called municipal bonds.

### What Goals Do They Satisfy?

Municipals have one major attraction over all other kinds of fixed-income paper: they are (for the most part) free of federal taxation, and if they have been issued in your home state, they are free of state and local taxes as well.

(Some of the income may be subject to the alternative minimum tax if the municipal bond is deemed to be a private activity bond. It may also be subject to calculations for those whose Social Security benefits exceed established levels where up to half becomes taxable income.)

### How Safe Are They?

General obligation bonds (GOs) are backed by the full faith, credit and taxing power of the municipality issuing them. For most towns and cities, that taxing power is based on real estate and land taxes, sales taxes and income taxes. The bonds need not be backed by real assets but rather by the knowledge that there is the political will to impose sufficient tax rates to finance the bonds. Most munis are GOs.

Revenue bonds pay bondholders from some specific source of funds—usually the activity for which the bonds raised money in the first place. Fees, charges and income stream are derived from a municipal activity, such as a garbage landfill or a parking garage. Thus, bond owners cannot rely on any general taxing power but rely only on the limited revenues from a specific activity.

The tax-free aspect of municipal bonds arises from the reciprocal immunity that sovereign taxing authorities extend to each other. States don't tax income from Treasury obligations, and the federal government does not tax income that comes from municipal bonds. States do, however, tax municipal bond income if it comes from another state.

Since munis are tax-free, they are issued with a lower rate of interest. At one time they paid only about 70 percent of what long-term Treasury bonds paid. Of late that gap has narrowed considerably. When municipal bonds are priced so that they yield almost as much as taxable government bonds, they are at a premium.


## What Do They Typically Cost?

To see how much tax-free income is worth in your tax bracket, follow this formula:

$$\frac{\text{Tax-exempt yield}}{100\% - \text{Tax bracket}}$$

Here is what a 7.5 percent muni bond is worth in the 28 percent bracket:

$$\frac{7.5\%}{100\% - 28\%} = \frac{7.5\%}{72\%} = 10.42\%$$

An investor must receive at least 10.42 percent from an equivalent taxable instrument to receive the same aftertax yield.

Municipal bonds are generally sold in denominations of $5,000, but it may be difficult to buy a few at a time. Institutions dominate the municipal bond market; therefore, individual investors must search for available inventory. Many small investors buy municipal bond funds: the funds issue shares between $10 and $25.

All munis are not equal, a fact that accounts for their different prices even if the coupon rates and maturity dates are the same. Though there are 40,000 municipal authorities issuing bonds, their issues generally fall into two categories: (1) general obligation bonds and (2) revenue bonds. After the crisis in the municipal market, when New York City declared a moratorium in the mid-1970s and the Washington Public Power Supply System defaulted in the early 1980s, investors are more cautious in evaluating the source of income to pay interest and principal.

## Where Are They Sold?

A vast number of municipal bonds are sold in the secondary market. Your broker will consult *The Blue List*, a publication of current municipal and corporate offerings. The daily newspapers publish only a few typical issues as a guide to prices. Full-service brokers usually have an inventory of municipal bonds for their customers.

## What Does It Cost To Buy and Sell Them?

If you buy municipal bonds, you are likely to buy them net, that is, the broker's commission is already in the price. The charge to purchase a bond is nominal, about $5 per bond.

## How Liquid Is the Market?

The 1986 Tax Reform Act has made life for municipal bond buyers more difficult. Bonds are now placed in one of four taxable categories: (1) bonds for essential services, where at least 90 percent of the bond proceeds are used for government purposes; (2) private activity bonds issued after August 7, 1986, where 10 percent or more of the bond proceeds benefit private entities; (3) taxable municipals; and (4) bonds issued before August 7, 1986, which remain tax-free. Remember that private activity bonds may be subject to the alternative minimum tax, and taxable municipals are taxable but have higher yields as a result.

Municipalities have also issued zero coupon bonds, which are issued at a deep discount from their face value. Unlike the Treasury zeros, no federal taxable income is imputed to them. Thus they are ideal for general accounts that are already tax advantaged.

Municipal bonds are considered extremely safe but are subject to the price fluctuations attendant with interest rate movements. When rates go up, the price of municipal bonds goes down. At one time, the municipal bond market did not fluctuate much; it was a sleepy backwater for institutional investors. Of late their tax-free aspects have drawn a great deal of attention in a world where taxation is a major consideration. The municipal bond market is not as liquid as the Treasury market. You may have to take a price concession if you wish to sell in a hurry, especially if the issue is not well known.

The municipal bond market is dominated by large players; it is hard for small investors to obtain small pieces and odd lots, let alone the basic information to make judgments. Therefore, municipal bond funds have attracted a great deal of attention.

### How Much Can You Make?

Long-term investors know the current yield and the yield to maturity when they purchase municipal bonds. While the yield is important, it is the aftertax yield that should be the major consideration in purchasing munis.

# CORPORATE BONDS

## What Are They?

In the private (nongovernmental) sector, a vast array of bonds is available. Very few corporations finance their needs with equity and short-term bank financing alone. Some companies, such as service companies, can if they have large cash flows and little need for capital investment. Others, such as telephone companies, manufacturing firms and utilities, require large sums for plant and equipment. The issues of debt come in a variety of forms other than plain vanilla. There are debentures, convertible bonds, sinking fund bonds, equipment trust certificates, mortgage bonds, income bonds, put bonds, junk bonds, floating-rate bonds (and notes) plus other oddities such as bonds with warrants, participation bonds, gold bonds and some European hybrids. Most of these will be explained in detail in *The Basics of Bonds*.

## What Goals Do They Satisfy?

For the moment, it is sufficient to note that they all represent some form of debt obligation—those who buy bonds become creditors of the corporation issuing the bonds. They do not participate in the profits, no matter how spectacular or extraordinary those may be. For the bondholder, bonds provide a high rate of return. The return is relatively risk-free if the corporate bonds are of investment grade.

## How Safe Are They?

To issue bonds, a company is obliged to issue an indenture or deed of trust describing the bonds and the promises that will legally bind it. The indenture, provided by legal counsel, explains the way repayment is to be made, the interest rate for the bondholder, what collateral will back the bonds and other conditions of the issue. The trustee, usually a bank or trust company, acts to protect the bondholders should the corporation get into trouble. Corporate bonds have no guarantee as to their safety, unlike the Treasury and municipal bond markets.

The actual bonds are now likely to be in registered form (ownership is recorded on the books of the corporation or issuing agency) rather than in bearer form (issued without an owner's name but with coupons that may be cashed by the possessor of the bond). Registered bonds make bookkeeping easier, and the government can more easily identify bond owners for tax purposes.

## What Do They Typically Cost?

Corporate bonds are generally issued in denominations of $1,000 and are quoted as a percentage of face value. Thus a bond selling at a discount, say at 95 percent, is priced at $950, and if at a premium of 120, or 120 percent of par value, then the price is $1,200. If you buy high coupon bonds when rates are low, the bonds will sell in excess or *premium* of their face value. Similarly, if you buy low coupon bonds when prevailing interest rates are high, they will be selling at a discount.

Prices of bonds are determined by three essential factors: (1) the coupon rate paid semiannually; (2) the maturity date on which a corporation repays the face value of a bond and redeems its promise; and (3) the prevailing interest rate. Other factors also affect a bond's price, such as the rating applied by one of the rating agencies and the general state of business for a particular corporation. Nevertheless, the three factors cited previously are clearly dominant.

This fluctuation in the price of bonds naturally changes the yield. A 10 percent coupon bond has a yield of 10 percent when the price is at the face value of $1,000. When the price of the bond falls to $900, the current yield is then about 11 percent. When the price advances to $1,100, the current yield is only 9 percent. The original buyer continues to have a fixed yield; it is only the new buyer who must calculate the actual yield rather than the coupon rate.

Furthermore, the yield to maturity also changes as the bond price moves around. One must figure the premium or the discount—that is, the capital loss or gain must be subtracted or added to the average percentage yield to arrive at the yield to maturity. (How to calculate yield to maturity is described in *The Basics of Bonds*.)


**Where Are They Sold?**

Both bearer and registered bonds are traded freely since there is a large secondary market. If you wish to buy corporate bonds, you will find a large representative list in the daily newspapers. New issues are announced in the financial press. Your broker should have no difficulty purchasing bonds of a new issue.


**What Does It Cost To Buy and Sell Them?**

The commission on corporate bonds, as with most fixed-income instruments, is small. The commission is approximately $5 per bond.

### How Liquid Is the Market?

Liquidity in the corporate bond market is uneven. Large and well known issues are easily traded. However, small corporate issues may be difficult to dispose of, and you may have to take a concession in the price.

### How Much Can You Make?

During the course of their long lives, bonds are likely to sell at a premium or discount depending on the interest rate weather. While institutions attempt to profit on the ups and downs of these interest rate moves, individual investors tend to buy them and forget them. Long-term investors receive their interest payments. If a bond has to be sold before maturity, an investor may suffer a loss if the prevailing interest rate is higher than the coupon rate. Conversely, if the prevailing rate is lower than the coupon rate, an investor will experience a gain.

# • 10 •

# *Mutual Funds and Money Market Securities*

## MUTUAL FUNDS

*Mutual funds*—either open-end or closed-end—are those funds organized by investment companies to invest pooled money from the public in the securities of other companies. Shares in an open-end mutual fund are bought or sold directly from the investment company or its sponsor and represent the actual net asset value of the fund.

### What Are the Advantages of Open-End Mutual Funds?

Mutual funds are best suited to investors who do not wish to commit either a great deal of time to security analysis or a great deal of money to the securities markets.

The typical open-end mutual fund (and at last count there were 1,580 stock and bond funds) encompasses shares of 50 to 500 different companies. There are no statutory limits as to how big an open-end mutual fund can be or to what size it can grow. Mutual funds are operated by investment management companies and brokerage houses. For their efforts, they are compensated in two ways: (1) by a onetime sales charge or load (typically between 4 and 8.5 percent), and/or (2) by an annual management fee (between 1/2 and 1 percent). Some investment management companies do not charge a sales fee, and their funds are called no-load funds.

## What Are the Advantages of Closed-End Mutual Funds?

Not as well known as its big brother (the open-end mutual fund), the closed-end fund serves a small but special niche of investors who like to buy the funds and forget them. Purchasers of closed-end funds are buying shares in a fixed pool of underlying companies. The management company first creates a portfolio of common stocks and then sells the public fractional interest or shares in that fixed pool. Unlike the open-end fund, the management company never redeems those issued shares. Instead, the shares are sold in the open market; some are even listed on the exchanges.

Therefore, shares of closed-end funds do not sell at their net asset value, but rather sell in accordance with supply and demand. Historically, closed-end funds sell at substantial discounts from their net asset values. Consequently, it does not seem profitable to buy them when they are first underwritten.

They can, however, be profitable if bought in the after-market, where it is possible to buy $100 of assets for $80 or $90. Furthermore, the discount means that there is a higher yield than that stated. Finally, funds bought at a discount have traditionally had better potential for gain on the upside and have had something of a floor on the downside. Not only does the discount disappear in strong bull markets, it also disappears in falling markets.

No one is quite sure why closed-end funds sell at a discount. Perhaps it is because there is no one out promoting them, unlike open-end mutual funds. The management company does little more than act as trustee. However, closed-end funds have lately attracted attention as some entrepreneurs have bought them with an eye to converting them to open-end funds and profiting thereby.

## What Goals Do They Satisfy?

Both open and closed funds have grown enormously in size because they offer professional management relatively cheaply to small investors. Today institutions dominate trading, and many people feel that the only way to fight fire is with fire—join a mutual fund and let the experts do it.

In addition, it is difficult to spread or diversify with a limited number of dollars. According to a New York Stock Exchange study, the average investor has less than $10,000 in the stock market—barely 100 shares of Johnson and Johnson and 200 shares of Kodak. With a fund, it is easy to have a fractional slice of 500 companies at one shot.

Moreover, it is possible to buy a mutual fund from a management company or brokerage house that runs a family of funds—from government bonds to global investments. Investors can easily and with only a modest bookkeeping charge (sometimes even at no charge) jump from one fund to another. Some families of funds are so large that one can even choose a sector (such as services, computers or biotechnology) or a country to invest in.

## How Safe Are They?

The mutual fund serves the purpose of safety through diversity and expert management. For small commissions and/or management fees, professional financial opinions and executions are available. There are many different kinds of mutual funds, and the records for performance run from excellent to poor. Mutual funds are not guaranteed, but the record of safety for the fund industry is very sound.

## What Do Shares Typically Cost?

By and large, shares of mutual funds are low, ranging between $1 and $25. They are purposely kept that way so that the funds are accessible to most investors.

## Where Are They Sold?

No-load funds are rarely sold through brokerage houses. Interested buyers of no-load funds must approach the management companies directly. (A guide to no-load funds may be obtained from the No-Load Mutual Fund Association Inc., 11 Pennsylvania Plaza, New York, NY 10001.) Brokerage houses sell either their own funds or funds that they recommend, and, of course, they can earn a commission on the sale of those funds.

## What Does It Cost To Buy Them?

The daily prices of mutual funds are listed in the newspapers and financial press. The *net asset value* (NAV) is the market value of all stocks divided by the number of shares outstanding. It is the price at which one can redeem shares from a management company. No-load funds do not charge a sales fee. However, some no-load funds have a "12b-1" fee, which is a charge for distribution and marketing that ranges from 0.25 percent to 1 percent annually.

Mutual funds that do charge a sales fee (load funds) often use sliding scales, depending on the size of the purchase. They may charge as much as an 8.5 percent commission for a small purchase of a few thousand dollars but only 3 percent for a $100,000 purchase. Some funds appear to have no sales charge, that is, they put all your money to work. But harbored in the fine print may be a *back-ended sales charge*—a sales commission charged when you sell shares before a specific period or one that is graduated downward as the holding period is extended.

## How Liquid Is the Market?

When you want to dispose of your shares in an open-end mutual fund, you simply sell them back to the company that issued them. Should everyone in a mutual fund try to redeem on the same day, there might be a liquidity problem. But like banks, most funds keep a sufficient amount of cash to stem such a run. Nevertheless, it is important to remember that except for a few money market funds, mutual funds do not have any depositor insurance. There have been few such problems in the mutual fund industry, but they are not unknown.

If you wish to sell the shares of a closed-end fund, you must find a buyer, since the investment company does not redeem the shares. If the fund is listed on an exchange, the transaction is easily accomplished. While there is no sales charge for a closed-end fund, there is a broker's commission for buying or selling the shares.

Critics of mutual funds do make some points that are worth considering. Mutual funds are not cheap: due to a substantial sales charge, a 12b-1 fee and an annual management fee, buyers are hardly getting a free ride. These charges will indeed reduce your rate of return.

Moreover, buying professional management skills may be overrated. In 1987 (not an atypical year) before the crash, the newsletter *Growth Fund Guide* (September 1987) asked "exactly how many U.S. funds outperformed the averages . . . the answer is only about 4 percent!" A few funds do have long, consistent and impressive records. But investors must weed those out of a vast number that perform at best indifferently. And the reason they perform in line with the market is simply that they are the market. By their nature and size, they must buy listed exchange companies; otherwise, they threaten to swamp the market for small OTC companies. Critics argue that individual investors may be at a disadvantage as to timing, information and resources. However, they can participate in markets that are virtually closed to the mutual funds.

Nevertheless, mutual funds can play a role in your investment portfolio if you have determined a fund's objectives and how it fits with your goals. If a fund has had reasonable success over a ten-year period in up and down markets, it could be an excellent selection, rather like an anchor to windward. Mutual funds are, at best, long-term holdings since they can be expensive to enter and exit. It is, of course, easy to move from one fund to another within a family of funds—and at times tempting. But investors should be cautious in undertaking such switching (even though telephone switch funds and newsletters have been in fashion lately) since there is little evidence that the average investor is likely to profit greatly from the activity.

### Load or No-Load Funds?

The inevitable question arises: Which group performs better, the load or no-load funds? There is little conclusive proof that investors obtain superior performance from load funds. There is, however, an endless debate, with both sides showing some outstanding records. Nonetheless, you should be quite certain that a fund meets the following objectives:

- The costs of operating (the expense ratio, which can run from 0.5 percent to 1.5 percent) are held down.
- The fund provides additional services (e.g., telephone redemption and checking).
- Annual turnover of the portfolio is not excessive (no more than 2/3 or 3/4 of the portfolio).
- The fund's track record is enviable—along with the consideration of a sales charge.

## MONEY MARKET SECURITIES

### What Are They?

*Money market funds* are open-end mutual funds (with no limit to their size) that buy various forms of indebtedness in large volume. The funds are then sold to individual investors in one-dollar denominations. Yields from the underlying investments are passed on to fund holders as interest (after deducting for management fees). While the portfolio mix varies with each money market fund, the funds generally contain bank CDs, commercial paper, bankers' acceptances and Treasury bills of short-term maturities. Some funds are tax-free since their portfolios are composed of municipal bonds. Individual investors cannot create their own money market funds since some of the components are sold in $100,000 or $1 million pieces.

### What Goals Do They Satisfy?

Money market funds are the most widely known type of mutual fund. They are created by investment management companies or brokerage houses. Originally developed in the 1970s as temporary depositories for funds to be used for investment purposes, money market funds now have a permanent life of their own, with hundreds of billions invested in them.

Investors now use money market securities to save money at the highest yields available. Your funds are instantly available in these demand accounts, though there might be some restrictions as to how many transactions you can make monthly.

## How Safe Are They?

Money market funds are quite safe. One or two had minor liquidity problems when the funds were new, but now maturity dates are kept short—between one and two months. In the junk-bond crisis of 1990, some funds had problems with a few junk-bond issues that defaulted. In theory, this could have reduced the value of those funds, and the investor's fractional interest. In reality, the investment companies stepped in to cover the losses so that investors suffered no loss. Most money market funds do not have junk bonds in their portfolios.

But there is a lesson: Any money market fund whose yield is dramatically different from the average of all funds should be suspect. Yields of money market funds are summarized once a week in the business press. Remember, there is no insurance or government guarantee for such funds, as there is for money market accounts in banks. If you require a government guarantee, your funds should be kept in a money market deposit account in a bank.

## What Do Shares Typically Cost?

Money market securities, whether funds or deposit accounts in banks, are always denominated in one dollar units. Interest accumulates and it accrues to the original principal. Since there is no sales charge, you obtain the highest yields readily available to investors who cannot afford to buy six-figure CDs, government bonds or commercial paper. There is a fractional management fee, but it is, in a sense, the price of admission to these securities.

## Where Are They Sold?

Money market funds are sold by a variety of investment companies. Brokerage houses also have in-house money market funds. Investors can arrange to have their credit balances swept into a firm's money market account while waiting for other investment positions.

These popular items are essentially forms of mutual funds made popular by the 1978–81 inflationary surge, when the rate of return on money market funds approached 17 percent for a short period of time. Many investors look back fondly on that period since they were also obtaining as much as 14 percent on CDs from their local banks. If the truth be known, they were hardly keeping ahead of inflation: in that environment their assets were depreciating every bit as fast as the interest they earned. It was, in short, a period that was destructive to monetary value.

## How Much Can You Make?

Money market funds only earn interest on the invested principal. Since the portfolios are constantly turning over, the interest rates are forever changing. Interest rates reflect the Treasury auctions and the prevailing interest rate market; thus, they change week by week.

Therefore, your principal does grow, but there is no predictability as to what interest you can earn over the near or far term. What is clear is that interest rates will tend to follow the rate for short-term money. Thus, these securities may not be suitable for individuals who need a predictable and fixed return on their funds.

While many investors long for those high yields that first put money market funds on the map, the conditions that made for those fleeting yields were not beneficial for assets. In the final analysis, investors do better when nominal interest rates are not sky-high. Or, to put it in a positive light, real interest rates (the nominal rate less the rate of inflation as measured by the *CPI*) are higher when there is not much inflation.

# • 11 •

# *Investing in Speculative Instruments*

## WHAT ARE THE ADVANTAGES?

Investing is often regarded as a stodgy, slow, conservative business. Perhaps that is as it should be—most often savings and investment funds are hard to acquire, and no one wants to see them squandered. The racetrack has its place with your entertainment buck but not with your hard-earned, serious money. In the last analysis, most crap-shooters crap out, and the casino almost always wins.

Investing and gaming are different. The former requires planning to obtain investments that are safe, provide an adequate return and are marketable. The latter requires an activity or happenstance, whether natural or artificial, that provides for a quick decision, a winner or loser. To be successful in investing, you need patience and knowledge. To be successful in wagering, you need Lady Luck and an absence of information (which serves only to confuse).

Is there a happy compromise? Probably not, in terms of economic purpose and personal objectives. But a number of investors have found that they can speed up the investing game and reduce its time frame so that what took place over months can now happen in days or weeks. While they are not gambling per se, they are now obtaining some of the immediacy that comes with games of chance. They have, in short, discovered the world of derivative instruments.

Derivative instruments are contracts or convertible securities that change in price along with and/or obtain much of their value from price movements in related or underlying securities or commodities. In other words, the price of gold bullion is the underlying issue in the gold market. Gold futures contracts—one of the derivative gold instruments—tend to fluctuate in price as related to the price of bullion.

## WHAT ARE THE DISADVANTAGES?

Derivative instruments change their prices rapidly. Moreover, they are purchased for relatively small down payments, that is, they are highly leveraged. A small price movement can quickly double the amount of money you actually put up, or conversely, it can reduce it in half. Therefore, your exposure to loss is very great, and your risk is great.

## OPTIONS: CALLS AND PUTS

### What Are They?

An *option* is a right to buy or sell 100 shares of a corporation's common stock at a fixed (or striking) price. This right has a limited life, usually 30, 60 or 90 days. Since options are listed on the exchanges, the dominant player is the Chicago Board Options Exchange (CBOE). By and large, options are listed for all the more active securities, either on the CBOE or the stock exchanges.

## What Goals Do They Satisfy?

In the last decade or so, options have become one of the hottest investment vehicles in the financial world. Their appeal stems from two factors. First, they are relatively cheap compared with the stock they represent. Their leverage (the use of borrowed funds) enables them to control underlying shares worth far more. Second, the potential for loss is limited to the price of the option. In brief, you can be sure that your selection will never cost more than the premium you paid for the option.

## How Safe Are They?

Since you cannot lose more than the original premium, options are one of the safest of derivative instruments. Buyers of options have two kinds of options to consider and at the least four alternatives to choose from. (Combinations of these basic positions are, of course, possible, leading to refinements of strategy and enhancement of choices.) There are call options and put options. A *call option* (or *contract*) allows a purchaser to literally "call away" from the seller of the option (another investor, trader or speculator) 100 shares at a predetermined price (the striking price) up to a certain date.

## What Do They Typically Cost?

For example, suppose an investor is certain that the Food and Drug Administration (FDA) will allow the Well-Being Pharmaceutical Company to sell its new ulcer drug within the next month or so. When that news is publicly confirmed, the investor expects a strong rise in the price of Well-Being's shares. At the moment, funds are tight, so instead of buying 100 shares at $50 ($5,000), the investor buys an at-the-money option (the strike price equals the market price of the underlying stock) for 60 days at 6.5 ($6.50 x 100), that is, a contract on 100 shares for $650.

### Where Are They Sold?

The investor buys the option through a brokerage house, which in turn executes the order on one of the exchanges. Let's assume that the investor's perceptions are accurate, the FDA cooperates and the shares appreciate to $60 before the option expires in 60 days. The option's price moves in lockstep with the underlying shares. After a breakeven point, the call-buyer (the purchaser of the option) sees that for every dollar advance in the shares, the option also moves a dollar. (Details and the arithmetic of option funding are dealt with extensively in *The Basics of Speculating*.) While the common stock moved 20 percent (from $50 to $60), the option moved 154 percent (from $6.50 to $16.50).

### What Does It Cost To Buy and Sell Them?

The commission costs to trade options are nominal, a few dollars per contract. The clear advantages are the ability to control $5,000 of stock for an initial $650 and the possibility of achieving a high percentage of gain. The disadvantages would become readily apparent if the FDA did nothing or approved the new drug in 90 days instead of in 60 days. An option is a "wasting" contract, and it becomes a little less valuable each day as it moves to expiration.

## How Liquid Is the Market?

Since option contracts are short-term instruments, a great deal of trading occurs. Therefore, the option markets are very liquid, and it is easy to sell or buy options without any price concession.

If the FDA declines to approve Well-Being's ulcer drug or if the market perceives that the drug is not that different from three other ulcer drugs and will not increase the company's share of the business, Well-Being's common stock will fail to advance. In this case, the option may be worthless upon expiration, a fact that should move the option holder to sell it before all value is gone.

The put option gives a buyer the right to sell 100 shares at a fixed price to the option seller. Let's assume that a put buyer is convinced that there is a glut of ulcer drugs and that the announcement of a new drug will not only cause no price increase but that the shares could fall in an anti-climax. By buying a put, the investor acquires the right (but not the obligation) to sell 100 shares at $50. If the put buyer is right, he or she will be able to get the option seller to take the shares at the higher price of $50, even though the market is substantially lower.

## How Much Can You Make?

In short, there are only two kinds of option contracts, calls and puts, and an investor can buy one or the other. He or she can also sell the options, that is, take the other side of the trade. Though less popular than buying, selling puts and calls assures the seller of a source of additional income for a portfolio, thereby raising its rate of return. Selling options is a way to increase a portfolio's yield. If the portfolio had no price appreciation throughout the year, the sale of options might increase the yield by 5 or 8 percent, depending on how aggressive the seller is.

Selling options reveals another side of the option business. Buying options appeals to those who want to speculate, who wish to inject a little more chance into their investment program. Selling or writing options, on the contrary, is a conservative way to protect profits and raise earnings from option premiums. Institutions are major sellers of options in an attempt to increase their investment performance. Individual investors can also participate in this side of the investment business.

## FUTURES: FINANCIAL, STOCK INDEX AND CURRENCY

### What Are They?

A *commodity* is another type of derivative instrument. Until recently, commodity (or futures) contracts were in a world rather removed from investment. The price of wheat and meat was of concern only to traders in Chicago or farmers in Kansas. All that has changed for a couple of reasons. The public is now concerned about the price of commodities, whether it be a barrel of oil, an ounce of gold or a pound of bacon. Inflation has made everyone price-conscious.

Furthermore, the investment world has borrowed a leaf from the commodity business by applying the idea of futures contracts to stocks, bonds and indices on stocks and bonds. To understand this transformation, a quick tour of a commodity or futures contract will help.

Farmers, mineral producers and manufacturers are in business to raise agricultural products, drill for oil and mine minerals, and produce finished products from raw materials. They can only do that if they have a reasonable idea as to their costs and selling prices. It is, of course, difficult to determine future events.

Some producers and farmers do not even try to predict future prices. They buy or sell in the cash (or spot) market, taking or paying whatever price prevails—and indeed, spot markets exist for most commodities. More than a century ago, however, farmers and producers shifted their pricing decisions from the future to the present. By entering into commodity contracts with investors, dealers and traders, they could fix their prices by agreeing to deliver or take delivery at a certain price at a certain time.

This solution transferred the risk of pricing from the farmers, miners and producers to those who were better situated to absorb financial risk—the financiers. Futures contracts called for a standardized product, a set quantity and fixed delivery dates. The contracts could then be sold and bought during their lifetimes—depending on the perceptions of the financial world. A drought in the wheat belt and a possible shortage of wheat would send prices skyrocketing. Conversely, a bumper crop and surpluses would send them reeling. Farmers didn't have to worry; they were guaranteed their contract price.

The speculators who dealt in the contracts had to worry, but they could hedge or offset their risks. If they were "long" (i.e., owned a contract that entitled them to buy the commodity), it was possible to "go short" (i.e., purchase a futures contract that entitled them to sell the commodity in question). In brief, financial techniques evolved to handle business risk—and handle it with flexibility and greater efficiency. Contracts in commodities have smoothed and rationalized what otherwise would have been erratic and wildly fluctuating markets.

This is not to say that the world of futures contracts is a hayride. Compared with the stock and bond markets, commodity trading can be fast and frenetic. It carries a high degree of risk, and fortunes are made and unmade in matters of hours.

## What Goals Do They Satisfy?

What makes commodities so alluring (and so dangerous) is the high degree of leverage in a futures contract. Participants need to put down only 5 or 10 percent of the value of the contract as earnest money. The full price for the contract is paid only upon actual delivery of the product. This need not concern the investor-speculator since most contract positions are terminated before delivery. The only people taking or making delivery are end users—for example, the producers of bread or the minters of gold coins. You will not have 112,000 pounds of sugar or 5,000 bushels of wheat delivered to your front door, if you inadvertently forget to close out a futures position.

To appreciate the leverage and the risk, take the standard gold contract for 100 troy ounces worth $45,000 ($450 per ounce × 100). If you had strong feelings that war, revolution, financial collapse or spiraling oil prices were imminent, you might go long on one or more gold contracts. A commodity dealer (and not all stock brokers deal in commodities) might require earnest money of 5 percent, or $2,250, as an initial deposit (or maintenance margin). If the price fell, you would be notified to put up more cash to keep the margin intact. If you did not respond, your contract would be terminated. Commodity contracts are priced to the market every day. If the market price of gold rises, the buyer will find that the price of the contract rises one dollar for every penny change in the price of gold. As with all commodity contracts, there is a daily limit to the price movement. In the case of gold, it is $25 per ounce.

The return on your initial investment can be far in excess of buying the actual bullion. For example, if the price of gold had moved to $475, your profit would be calculated as follows: selling price ($47,500) less the purchase price ($45,000) or $2,500. If the initial deposit was $2,250, the return would be as follows:

$$\frac{\$2,500}{\$2,250} = 111\%$$

This compares nicely with an increase of 5.5 percent, the increase in the spot market for gold. Bear in mind that if the market had indeed moved to $425 per ounce, you would have lost your initial margin and your position unless you had met the margin call.

## How Safe Are They?

The combination of volatility and leverage makes futures trading extremely risky and hardly for the faint of heart. More importantly, among nonprofessionals, nine out of ten people lose money rather than make it in commodities. In short, commodity contracts are anything but safe.

## What Do They Typically Cost?

Commodity contracts come in all sorts of differing sizes. The total value of a contract may be $50,000 or $100,000, but a speculator only puts up a few thousand dollars to secure the contract. In short, the actual earnest money may be only 5 or 10 percent of the value of the contract. However, the speculator is responsible for shouldering the total losses should the market turn the wrong way.

## Where Are They Sold?

Futures brokers specialize in the trading of commodities. Some full-service brokers also transact commodity business, but many discount brokers do not. They clear their order executions through the appropriate exchanges—those ones that deal in a particular commodity. Gold, for example, is traded on the New York Commodity Exchange, while wheat is traded on the Chicago Board of Trade.

## What Does It Cost To Buy and Sell Them?

Futures commissions are extraordinarily cheap. Futures brokers will execute a round turn—both the buying and the selling—for as little as $25 or $50.

## How Liquid Is the Market?

The commodities markets are quite liquid, especially in their active phases. Futures contracts have daily limits, a technique that acts to cool excited or speculative markets. Nevertheless, a move to the daily limit might well jeopardize the original investment.

To counter this disadvantage yet participate in this high-stakes game, it is possible to join one of the mutual funds devised exclusively for commodities. Another way is to purchase a limited partnership in a managed account program. Both these approaches are likely to improve your chances, since full-time professionals are better able to hedge their trades and limit losses.

## How Much Can You Make?

As noted earlier, the allure of the futures markets is their enormous leverage, which allows for the doubling and tripling of invested capital in relatively short order. You can, in brief, make a killing with gains of 100 or 1,000 percent. But, of course, you can also lose equivalent sums.

## FINANCIAL FUTURES: HEDGING YOUR BETS

In the 1970s, the investment world took the trading techniques associated with commodities and applied them to stocks and bonds. The new creations, which constitute a virtual revolution in financial devices, fall into three categories: (1) interest rate futures, (2) stock index futures and (3) foreign currency futures. These financial futures contracts have overwhelmed all the older agricultural and mineral commodity contracts.

The reason for developing financial futures was essentially defensive—to protect interest-sensitive assets from the fluctuations of interest rates. Remember the basic law of fixed-income investments: When interest rates go up, the value of fixed-income debt goes down, and vice versa. Institutions started to use Treasury bond futures to hedge their portfolios of bonds—against either falling or rising interest rates.

A hedge in the futures business is a form of protection from adverse price movements. Players in the futures markets consist of two parties: hedgers and speculators. It is the hedgers (banks, insurance companies and private individuals) who have a portfolio position to protect by usually being short futures contracts. This is called a long hedge since they are protecting an already established (long) position.

Should Treasury bonds fall in value because of rising interest rates, futures contracts (which are $100,000 per contract) will fall in price as well. Thus the loss in the long position is made up by an equal and opposite gain in the short position. Speculators, who have no position to protect, buy the futures contract. By taking the opposite side of the trade, they hope to profit by guessing the right direction of interest rate movements.

These interest rate futures are available for Treasury bills, Treasury bonds, CDs and Eurodollars, among others. Every day they trade in tens of thousands of contracts— worth $1 million in Treasury bonds or $100,000 in Ginnie Maes. While the government does not guarantee a futures contract, the underlying paper is federal paper, so there is no question of value or delivery since these contracts are traded on the major commodity exchanges.

Unlike agricultural commodities, the financial futures markets can be used to take delivery of these financial instruments. Their appeal is enormous leverage—the margin on Treasury bills can be as little as 2 percent. A correct guess on interest rate movement can be extraordinarily profitable.

## STOCK INDEX FUTURES

If interest rate futures can give additional protection to fixed-income portfolios, will futures on stock indexes provide similar protection for equity? The financial world has developed futures contracts on all the major indexes— Standard & Poor's 100, Standard & Poor's 500, New York Stock Exchange Composite Index, American Stock

Exchange Major Market Index and the Value Line Composite Stock Index.

Each index is of a different size, composition and weighting. For example, the Standard & Poor's 500 stock index future is 500 times the index for whatever month is being quoted. If the index is at 330, the value of a contract is $165,000 (330 × $500). A buyer (or seller) of such a futures contract will have to put up approximately 7 percent as initial margin ($11,550). Traders with smaller appetites can buy the Standard & Poor's 100 or one of the less expensive indices.

Buying or selling a stock index future can protect a portfolio of stocks by acting as a contrary force. In brief, you can hedge your bets. If you have an established long portfolio, selling stock index futures will presumably give you downside protection. The futures contract is a substitute for the whole market: as your long portfolio falls and loses value, the futures contract gains in value, thus neutralizing the decline.

If you buy stock index futures without a portfolio to hedge, you are leaving yourself open and unprotected to the whims of the market. In erratic daily moves, you may well face a margin call if you are acting as a speculator rather than as a hedger. Stock index futures can be a high-stakes game, perhaps best left to professional speculators and traders. If, however, you have a better sense of market direction than you exhibit in picking stocks, these futures might be profitable.

## CURRENCY FUTURES

Contracts in foreign currency have grown with popularity as the economy becomes more internationalized. Currency futures are no different from other commodity contracts, except the product under consideration is 25,000 British pounds, 125,000 Swiss francs or one of a half-dozen frequently traded currency contracts.

These contracts are traded on a number of American as well as foreign exchanges. They originally appealed to business people who were obliged to hedge their foreign exchange exposure. For example, an importer contracts for a shipment of Swiss chocolate to be paid in three months' time. The importer buys a Swiss futures contract long, which gives him or her 125,000 Swiss francs at 65 cents per franc.

There is an exchange risk with a hedge on only one side. If the franc goes up to 70 cents (i.e., if the dollar falls), the importer makes money. But what if it falls to 60 cents (i.e., the dollar strengthens)? To hedge, the importer simultaneously sells short a Swiss franc futures contract at the same level of 65 cents. Thus, regardless of which way the price moves in the foreign exchange market, the importer will acquire the Swiss francs at the price originally intended, plus commission costs.

Investors who believe they have a sense of the direction of foreign exchange can enter the futures markets to buy or sell currency contracts. Like all futures, these contracts present a great deal of leverage, since many currency contracts can be negotiated with only a 4 percent margin down payment. In the case of the Swiss franc contract of 125,000 francs, at 65 cents the contract is worth $81,250. Traders need little more than $3,250 to buy (or sell) this contract. Leverage is also apparent in a one-cent move—that changes the value of the contract by $1,250.

All these futures contracts are highly risky and should be avoided by enthusiastic but innocent investors. They should also be ignored by people of moderate or limited resources. Indeed, most responsible commodity dealers will request a financial profile to see if the potential investor can withstand the possible losses involved with commodity trading. If, however, you have the resources, strong nerves and a keen sense of markets, futures can be exciting and profitable. Just remember one sobering fact: nine out of ten commodity speculators lose on any given trade, or to put it another way, 90 percent or more of the profits go to 10 percent of the traders.

## Y•O•U•R   M•O•V•E

- Analyze the various investment vehicles with regard to your personal situation. How do they fit your investment goals?
- Consider the financial instruments from the point of view of risk. Can you live (and sleep) with all the intended components of your portfolio?
- Draw up a list of your impending savings and investment choices.
- Assign a percentage of your assets to each category, depending on your sensitivity to risk.

# • 12 •

## *Do You Want To Be an Active or Passive Investor?*

### WHY BE A PASSIVE INVESTOR?

Money is an emotional subject. An old cliche suggests that fear and greed dominate the scene, excluding calm thought and rational judgment. It's better to leave it to someone else, someone less involved. Even if it costs money—the 1 or 2 percent annual fee that professional management charges—it is a service that is more than worthwhile. Professionals are capable of the one thing most investors cannot achieve: emotional distance from the funds over which they have discretion. This quality of disinterest can be critical to the investment process. If you are too emotionally or psychologically involved with your funds, or too nervous or apt to act prematurely or erratically, consider assuming a passive status as an investor. Indeed, even some professional money managers divorce themselves from their daily activities by letting other people handle their funds.

In addition, if you are going to be an active investor, you must spend time and energy familiarizing yourself with new events, monitoring the financial scene and planning your next steps. You must be disciplined and dedicated if you are to manage your own portfolio actively. If you cannot commit yourself to the level of effort needed for successful money management, there is nothing wrong with letting the experts do it for you.

## CHOOSING AN INVESTMENT COUNSELOR

Personal financial services are expensive, and investment counseling firms frequently require portfolios of $50,000 or $100,000 as a minimum for management. There is no easy guide to the selection of an investment adviser, but here are a few things to consider:

- Have they been in business for a while?
- Do they share your investment goals and understand your risk limitations?
- What kind of documented performance record can they show?
- Do they charge your account based on the amount of assets under management (as is the trade practice) or on some other basis?

A few firms will evaluate money managers. One of the more successful ones is RCB International of Stamford, Connecticut.

## CHOOSING APPROPRIATE FUNDS

More modest holdings can be well served by mutual funds; some, in fact, are operated by investment counseling companies.

The most obvious choice for you as a passive investor is the selection of an investment management company that operates a number of different mutual funds. Investment companies issue their own shares to investors and in turn invest those proceeds in shares of public corporations.

If you are a passive investor, you want professional managers who provide superior results in the areas of interest to you. Their records of achievement are evaluated by Weisenburger & Co., Lipper Analytical Securities Corporation, *Barron's, Forbes, Fortune* and a number of newsletters dedicated to the mutual fund industry. These services and magazines are available in most libraries or for a modest fee.

There is no shortage of information concerning the performance of over 2,500 mutual funds. Information concerning other registered investment companies—unit investment trusts, closed-end funds and face amount certificate companies—is available but harder to come by, since they are less popular. For additional information, contact this trade association: the Investment Company Institute, 1775 "K" Street, Washington, DC 20006.

The passive investor should be cautious about evaluating one-year performance records and should look at long-term trends to see how a fund performs under adverse conditions and in bear markets. Many investment companies offer a family of funds, and for a nominal fee, an investor can switch objectives and/or sectors. This is convenient when you wish to move from stocks to bonds, or vice versa.

Nevertheless, it is difficult—even for professionals— to judge the major trends in markets. Mutual funds have performed in a superior fashion when left untouched (but not unmonitored) if they constantly rank in the upper quarter of all funds. Mutual fund investors have done remarkably well when invested in the right sectors, such as the gold funds in the late 1970s and the energy funds in the period 1979–82. The monitoring is equally as important as the initial selection since in subsequent years, both gold and energy have fallen from their highs.

## DO YOU WANT TO MANAGE YOUR OWN INVESTMENTS?

One of the major reasons for failure in money management is the lack of realistic objectives. What can rationally be expected is often quite different from the hyped anticipation created in the public mind. To be successful in the financial world, you need to be aware of historical precedents, the average return on savings, the rate of return on investments and normal yields—in short, you must appreciate the milestones that measure your speed and direction.

It is also important to recognize the aberrant, the abnormal and the singular occurrence. All too often investment decisions are little more than gut feelings made at the kitchen table from information culled from the morning newspaper or the evening TV news. When financial items are reported in the popular media, the news is likely to be either wildly optimistic or indubitably depressing—that, of course, is the nature of news. Acting on breaking news is generally a mistake.

What you can realistically expect in the world of finance depends on a number of critical factors, but overwhelmingly on the following factors:

- The time period involved
- The financial instrument and/or type of account
- The levels of risk you are willing to assume, both financially and psychologically

Other factors that contribute to investment success are no less important—namely, timing, access to information, knowledge and reasonable execution—but they only pave the road.

Most investors (and there are close to 50 million of them, according to a recent survey by the New York Stock Exchange) and potential investors consider the act of investing as something akin to saving. Put a little bit of money and/or stock away for a rainy day or a future occasion. There is, for the most part, little rhyme or reason inherent in most people's investment decisions, whether they are making their first or their fiftieth transaction. This chaotic approach usually leaves an erratic record of occasional runs, some hits and lots of errors.

## What Will It Require?

Successful management of money requires some planning, a bit of homework and a sense of goals or objectives. Instead of a random, haphazard and an occasional involvement with the financial world, the investor (whether neophyte or not) must exercise more than a little discipline.

Most successful investors consider their investments as a small, separate business—another profit center in their personal holding company. When investing is viewed from this angle, a consistent purpose and a disciplined orientation help ensure profits. In brief, you must work at it; there is no shortcut to investment success. Some years ago in the 1960s, professional money managers adopted a fad that can be summed up by their outlook—the "Nifty-Fifty." Only 50 or so businesses (out of a corporate universe of nearly 50,000 companies) were considered for their portfolios. This in turn led to the philosophy of the "One-Decision Stock," one that could be bought and forgotten.

As with most fads, this silliness passed. No great irreversible harm was done from this myopic policy, but it illuminated the fantasy of making once-and-for-all investment decisions. As in any other undertaking, the doors open on a new day every day, presenting both constant challenges and opportunities.

## HOW TO CHOOSE A BROKER

Perhaps the easiest way to begin an investment program is to begin as a passive investor. If the investment process holds out further interest for you, you can then move to becoming an active investor. Start with a mutual fund selected for its ability to match your objectives and risk tolerances. You might initially wish to select an aggressive fund in order to experience capital growth. Continue as a passive investor if you do not have the time or temperament to be an active investor. If you remain a passive investor, start investing in another mutual fund with a goal of income and safety to hedge your exposure. As you become more affluent, a municipal bond fund will provide extra tax-free income.

When you feel ready to become an active investor, select a goal or objective for your portfolio, whether income or growth, keeping your family and personal situation in mind. Your holdings should be diversified both in security selection and in time. Diversification will protect you against the ups and downs of the economic cycle, the ebb and flow of interest rates and the fortunes of business.

It is important to select the right brokerage house and the appropriate broker. A full-service brokerage house will provide you with investment ideas, detailed research, financial planning, special cash management accounts and a large inventory of products. For these services (whether you use them or not), the commission costs are likely to be high.

Discount brokerage firms offer only a few services. Their brokerage rates are considerably lower than those of full-service firms. They tender no advice and only execute orders for customers who know their own minds.

If you feel that you need guidance and/or information, a full-service broker is probably a better choice. After deciding on a firm you must select a broker within the firm. Personal recommendations are usually best. If that is not available, you can visit the firm and talk to a number of brokers. If you make your needs known, the firm may be able to help you select the right broker.

The history of the equities markets over the last hundred years shows a long, upward revaluation of common stock, interrupted by sharp and erratic setbacks. There is little reason to believe that that pattern will change as long as American productivity and ingenuity predominate. Investors are likely to be successful in pursuing a strategy of long-term equity investing. Not only will their capital appreciate, but they will increase purchasing power in the face of continuing inflation.

Active investors should also think about an America in transition, one in which global competition places the domestic economy under strain as a result of federal deficits, trade imbalances and an overpriced dollar. In a less-than-rosy scenario, the active investor (as well as the passive one) must consider a defensive strategy, one primarily emphasizing safety and income. Since neither investors nor anyone else can foresee economic developments, it is important to be prepared for all contingencies.

# • 13 •

## *Setting Up a Portfolio That's Right for You*

There is no "right" way to invest; many different profitable paths exist. Much depends on assets, age, income, family situation, career potential and a host of other factors. There are, of course, as many different ways to fail as there are ways to succeed. Greed, inattention, hot tips, fads and just plain bad timing can decimate a portfolio. However, with care, balance, diversification and suitable hedges, a long-term investor is likely to be treated very kindly by his or her investments.

Perhaps the easiest way to initiate an investment program is to begin as a passive investor. If the investment process holds out further interest for you, then move to becoming an active investor. Start with a mutual fund selected for its ability to match your objectives and risk tolerances.

You might initially wish to select an aggressive fund in order to experience capital growth, the essence of the stock market. Continue as a passive investor if you do not have the time or temperament to be an active investor. If you remain a passive investor, start investing in another mutual fund with the goal of income and safety to hedge your exposure. As you become more affluent, a municipal bond fund will provide extra tax-free income.

When you feel ready to become an active investor, select a goal or objective for your portfolio, whether income or growth, keeping in mind your family and personal situation.

## GROWTH PORTFOLIOS

As we have seen, there are a wide variety of investment instruments. Let's assume your objective is growth. The following instruments may fulfill your requirements:

- Common stock
- Options
- Convertible securities
- Futures contracts
- Deep discount bonds

Then consider your risk profile: Are you risk-averse, risk-neutral or a risk-lover? If you are risk-averse, you will immediately rule out futures contracts as too speculative. Options will also not be bought, but you might consider selling them for additional premium income. Perhaps you will decide to divide your funds equally between common stock and convertible bonds.

In either instance, examine the financials of the companies involved and the credit ratings assigned by rating agencies such as Standard & Poor's or Moody's to see that the issues pass muster. If you are risk-averse, insist on investment-grade quality—the first three rankings (A+, A, A–) for common stock and the first four ratings (AAA, AA, A, BBB) for convertible bonds.

If you are risk-neutral, you will probably avoid futures contracts, though you might consider buying some options to give your holdings a fillip. You are, after all, interested in growth of principal. Instead of dividing your funds equally between common stock and convertible bonds, consider allocating three-quarters of your funds to common stock and the remainder to convertible bonds. Also assess the quality of your common stock purchases. You might investigate secondary issues that are not blue chips to find faster growth issues.

If you are a risk lover, the world is your oyster, but discretion is always apropos. Perhaps 10 percent of your portfolio can be devoted to commodity contracts, an equal amount to options and the balance to the stock market. To avail yourself of the broadest growth selections, consider the new issue market, stocks listed on the OTC market and listed securities that have a history of rapid growth.

## Diversification and Time

Regardless of your risk profile, your holdings should be diversified both in security selection and in time. Diversification will protect you against the ups and downs of the economic cycle, the ebb and flow of interest rates and the fortunes of business. In brief, diversification gives you balance and safety.

Remember that successful investment programs are inevitably long-term. If you expect to make a "quick killing" in the stock market, your performance is likely to suffer. The risk lover can expect more immediate performance in the portion of the portfolio devoted to futures contracts and options since these instruments by their nature are short-term.

Table 13.1 shows sample distributions for growth portfolios arranged by risk.

**TABLE 13.1**  Sample Distributions for Growth Portfolios by Risk

| Category | Risk-Averse | Risk-Neutral | Risk Lover |
|---|---|---|---|
| Money market/T-bills | 10% | 5% | 5% |
| Common stock | 30 | 65 | |
| Bonds and convertible securities | 45 | 20 | |
| Deep discount bonds | 10 | 5 | 25 |
| Options | 5 | 5 | 10 |
| Futures | | | 10 |

## How Much To Invest

To maintain a relatively safe investment program, you must be diversified. Diversification is a function of money. Therefore, remain in mutual funds until you can muster enough funds to buy at least six different issues, preferably ten. You can, of course, buy odd lots (less than 100 shares) instead of the usual round lots (100 shares). That is slightly more expensive since there is an additional fractional charge for odd lots.

The amount of money needed clearly depends on the price of the issues. Shares on the New York Stock Exchange on average exceed $50 per share, while shares on the OTC market are frequently under $10 per share. While there are no hard rules, you probably should have a minimum of $5,000 or $10,000 to invest to give yourself sufficient balance.

## INCOME PORTFOLIOS

Income investors have a wider selection of investment vehicles than do growth investors. The following are some of the instruments involved in investing for income:

- U.S. Treasury securities
- U.S. agency securities
- Municipal bonds
- Corporate bonds
- Convertible securities
- Common stocks
- Money market mutual funds
- Certificates of deposit
- U.S. savings bonds

If you are investing for income, you are probably risk-averse or risk-neutral. It is also a reasonable assumption that you are somewhat older and concerned with your future income stream. Which of all these instruments do you choose?

If you are risk-averse, U.S. Treasury bills, notes and bonds give you total protection. U.S. agency paper is almost equally as safe. Municipal bonds, especially general obligation bonds, have a negligible default rate. In addition, they provide tax-free income.

If you are risk-neutral, corporate bonds, convertible securities and money market funds are acceptable. There is some risk—none have any guarantee. The corporate bonds and convertibles should be examined and their credit ratings noted to avoid any issues that are below investment grade.

Common stock deserves special consideration. Many issues, especially those of rapidly growing companies, pay no dividends. But there are many fine corporations that do pay dividends frequently yielding 5, 6 or 7 percent or more. Moreover, many companies have paid dividends for decades and are reluctant not to pay them even when business is poor. And some companies, particularly the utilities and telephone companies, attempt to raise their dividends on a regular basis.

With common stock, it is possible to have a decent stream of income, plus the potential for capital growth. While the latter is not an immediate concern for income investors, it should be. Common stock can offer a higher total return (dividends plus growth) than any other investment vehicle. Some portion of any portfolio should be dedicated to growth—and if it can provide income, so much the better. No portfolio is immune to higher taxes and the eroding nature of inflation. It is worth remembering that your 1980 assets were worth only about half in purchasing power in 1991. They can only remain constant if their purchasing power remains intact. Dividend-paying common stock is one of the ways of achieving that end.

### How Much To Invest

The obvious answer is the more, the better. In practice, the highest yields are restricted to jumbo CDs and other debt instruments that require $100,000 per investment. Happily, the modest investor can obtain almost the highest rates by either using money market funds or by extending the maturity of investment vehicles. The highest yields are generally reserved for the longest maturities. You will obtain more annual income with a 30-year Treasury bond than with a 1-year Treasury bill, all other things being equal.

Income investors must also consider the tax aspect of their income. Municipal bonds are certainly worthwhile if you are in a higher tax bracket. And saving in a retirement account allows for the accumulation of nontaxable income. There are limitations as to how much pretaxed income can be directed into a pension account; but whatever the limitation, take full advantage of this tax-free income depository.

Table 13.2 shows you sample distributions for income portfolios arranged by risk.

**TABLE 13.2**   Sample Distributions for Income Portfolios by Risk

| Category | Risk-Averse | Risk-Neutral |
|---|---|---|
| Savings bonds/CDs | 10% | |
| Money market/T-bills | 10 | 10% |
| T-bonds | 25 | 10 |
| Agency bonds | 20 | |
| Mutual funds | | 15 |
| Common stock | 15 | 25 |
| Corporate bonds/preferred stock | | 15 |
| Municipal bonds | 20 | 25 |

# • 14 •

## *Some Sample Portfolios*

The examples that follow represent a series of typical situations an individual or a family is likely to pass through in the course of a lifetime. Whether or not you make these passages, it is possible to glimpse alternate strategies. The personal tactics you use to implement these strategies will, of course, be based on your personal decisions; however, the tactics of the following investors might prove instructive.

### PORTFOLIO 1: SINGLE

Don had practiced dentistry for five years. He was quite successful in his inner-city practice, setting up shop in a gentrified storefront that used to be a butcher shop. While his earnings were substantial, his cash flow was a puzzlement. The reason for concern was his substantial debts, which stemmed from professional school, setting up an office and buying the expensive high-tech tools of the trade, not to mention his own personal indulgences. His accounts receivable were cleared through a local bank checking account.

Not much could be done about his contractual debts, but he did manage to combine them by refinancing them into one loan that lowered his monthly payments, even though it extended the debt payment a number of years. He also switched his receivables from a non-interest-bearing account to a money market deposit account to earn some interest on his cash balances.

Looking toward the future, Don decides that he would like to retire in 30 years. Therefore, for 15 years he plans to invest aggressively, taking on substantial risk. He will start with some aggressive mutual funds. After half a dozen years, he will liquidate the funds and actively take charge of his portfolio, concentrating almost solely on common stocks and occasionally buying options. For the second 15 years, he plans to invest with an eye toward income. To give his investment program some balance, he decides to use his Keogh retirement account for tax-deferred growth.

Under the new Keogh rules (based on the 1986 Tax Reform Act), Don can place $7,979 a year into a self-directed account. Not wishing to take on any risk with this portion of his earnings, he buys zero coupon Treasury bonds maturing in 15 years, and he expects to do that every year. With the prevailing rates at 8 percent, he calculates that he can lock up 23 bonds at $300 each. Within 15 years the bonds will have more than tripled. Like the plans of all of us, Don's plans are subject to change if he marries and starts a family. For the immediate future, he has a workable scheme that will start a lifelong investment portfolio.

## PORTFOLIO 2: MARRIED COUPLE WITH CHILD, ONE INCOME

Other than hanging, nothing concentrates the mind like having a new baby, especially the first one. Whatever else a child brings (such as happiness, amusement, warmth and love), it always brings bills—lots and lots of bills. Tom never considered that he was living in a fool's paradise, but he and Diana were submerged by the volume and amount of monthly invoices after Tom Jr.'s birth.

As a modest, one-income family with an income of $30,000 from Tom's job as an assistant buyer at a department store, Tom and Diana quickly came to the realization that some financial planning was in order if they were to reach their goal—a family of three children.

The bills from the obstetrician, hospital, nurse and diaper service were certainly sizable. But what really struck fear into their hearts was a small item in the evening paper from the Department of Agriculture that estimated it would take between $81,000 and $200,000 to raise one child from birth to 18 years of age. The sum was staggering—and that was before any allowance for college expenses.

They had fortunately received a small but noteworthy inheritance from Tom's aunt. Fifty thousand dollars was not overwhelming, but it was certainly welcome. The inheritance came in the form of common stock in two electric utility companies and in one telephone company, plus $20,000 in cash.

Rather than immediately move to a larger home, they decided to keep the stock since it has a good yield and presents no tax problem (other than the declared income) until it is sold. They put half the $20,000 into an aggressive growth fund. The other half went into a government agency mutual fund so that they will receive a high monthly yield that, along with the stock dividends, will help pay for the children's bills.

## PORTFOLIO 3: COUPLE — TWO INCOMES, NO BABY ON BOARD

For many people, serious financial planning does not start until marriage. Jake, age 37, and Cathy, age 34, were career-driven individuals totally caught up in self-advancement. Their relationship turned into marriage—the first for each.

Jake and Cathy were mindful that the good times might not always roll. Pundits after the October 1987 massacre predicted doom, gloom and another Great Depression. Could they possibly be right? While they did not cut back severely on their spending and consumption, Jake and Cathy decided that saving between 2 and 4 percent of their annual salary was too little, considering they jointly earned close to six figures.

What money they had accumulated was mixed up in U.S. savings bonds, a money market deposit account at their local bank and income savings plans at their respective jobs. When they finally agreed to do a little planning, they decided to make the purchase of a condominium their five-year goal.

Their first step was to increase their savings to $10,000 per year. They liquidated the $15,000 they had in savings bonds, which were paying only 6 percent a year. Furthermore, they reduced the amount of money in their money market account so that it held only two months' worth of income.

Jake and Cathy now have a nest egg of $40,000, which they have invested, half in zero coupon junk bonds—deeply discounted bonds that appreciate by 14 percent a year. At this rate, they will double that money in five years, before taxes. With the other half, they have bought quality growth stocks. To be on the safe side, they have taken all their income savings out of equity and have placed it into fixed-income funds. They have no guarantee about the depression, but within a few years they should have sufficient funds for a down payment on a condo, plus an anchor in their retirement accounts.


## PORTFOLIO 4: MIDDLE-AGED FAMILY—HIGHER EDUCATION, HIGHER TUITION

Timothy and Mary had arrived, so to speak. As a sales engineer for a large mainframe computer company, Timothy had prospered far above the dreams of his blue-collar parents. In his good years, salary and commissions exceeded $125,000. Living in an elegant suburb of Philadelphia, he and Mary had raised a large family of eight children. The last child, however, was born with Down's syndrome. While Timothy's income might have been sufficient in normal times, the expense of special medical and nursing care for their last child threw their college preparation plans into turmoil. Caught between rising medical costs and escalating educational expenses, Timothy and Mary had to take their first hard look at their financial resources.

At first, their immediate reaction to the problem of college costs was simple: the children would all go to college, but they would attend state schools. Upon the advice of their accountant, however, they decided to give their children some $70,000 that they had saved over their 20 years of marriage. While not quite as beneficial in tax terms as it would have been before the new tax code, it does lower the taxable income that Timothy and Mary derive from interest and dividends. They have opened separate accounts of $10,000 for each college-bound child (half cash, half stock) without any tax consequence to either the parents or the children.

Under the new 1986 Tax Reform Act, children under 14 are taxed at the same level as their parents. Timothy and Mary have devised a simple plan. For the children below 14 years of age, they have stressed rapid growth of principal by investing in growth stocks and tax-free income—in other words, stocks that pay no dividend and some U.S. savings bonds that increase in value, tax-free. They have also bought some single premium life insurance policies since these policies also compound on a tax-free basis and can later be used as a source of borrowed funds.

For their children over 14 years of age, their plans are somewhat different, since they are taxed in their own right. Timothy and Mary have shifted from total growth and tax-free accumulation to 50 percent income and the balance in quality growth. By shifting to high-yielding instruments—medium-grade bonds, collateralized mortgage obligations and some blue-chip stocks—they have a number of years to accumulate funds at a very low tax rate.

## PORTFOLIO 5: THE DIVORCE — ASSET SHIFTING, INCOME SHARING

Evelyn and Martin had come to the end of their marriage because of Martin's philandering. Evelyn greeted Martin's confession and desire to start divorce proceedings with some shock. After all, there were three children to worry about. When the news finally hit home, she realized that after 17 years of marriage, she was unable to support herself. Her teacher's license in another state had lapsed.

Beyond the first order of business, which for Evelyn was reentering the job market, was the problem of disposing of their joint property. This was clearly a legal issue to be reconciled by their attorneys. While fairness may well be in the eye of the beholder, both Martin and Evelyn wished to have an equitable separation for the benefit of the children. Concern for their children's well-being led them to a novel solution to their main asset, which was the cooperative apartment they had purchased some years ago at the "inside" price.

Instead of Martin alone moving out, both parents have taken separate apartments while the children remain in the nest. They feel that the idea of nesting is far less disturbing to the kids and that it's far easier for the parents to pop in and out than for the three kids to move each week.

This form of joint custody has solved the problem of what to do with the appreciated property—namely, do nothing and let it appreciate some more. As a well-paid television producer, Martin is able to afford both rents plus the co-op maintenance. However, both realize that it would be more equitable for Evelyn to share in and eventually be responsible for her own upkeep. Therefore, they have agreed to a sliding scale of maintenance: for every $1,000 Evelyn earns over $20,000, Martin reduces his payments by $500. Child support will continue until each child reaches majority.

Their financial assets had all been held in joint-tenant-with-right-of-survivorship accounts. This made it relatively simple to divide their securities in half. But Martin was leery of Evelyn's future entanglements as she was of his. In order for their children to inherit, the lawyers were instructed to set up separate living trusts with the joint property. In this way, should either parent die after starting another family, his or her earlier assets would go solely to their joint children, not to the estate that might be obliged to distribute to their second family as well.

Evelyn has kept most of the fixed-income assets—the municipal bond fund and the utilities and telephone companies—to give her some stable income. Martin, on the other hand, has taken the aggressive OTC issues and the rapidly growing, non-dividend-paying listed securities since he can both withstand the risk and write off losses against his income.


## PORTFOLIO 6: MIDLIFE CRISIS — STARTING OVER

Mark was the sales manager of Softouch, a computer programming company that specialized in banking and accounting applications. After 21 years with the firm and a number of promises of a vice presidency, he found himself edged out by a coworker. After a night's sleep, he decided to resign. Better to jump, he reasoned, before you're pushed. As an early baby boomer, he was surprised to find that he qualified for the company's pension plan. He never did understand some of the company's fringe benefits such as deferred compensation, the salary reduction plan and income savings.

His salary had always been his chief concern, but now it dawned on him that his benefits were worth about 20 percent of his earnings. Before he jumped ship, it was imperative to find out what he was entitled to. In addition, he was faced with the dilemma of quitting (and losing unemployment benefits) or being fired (and having to live with dismissal for cause on his resume). Either way, it was time to calculate his net worth and his unseen benefits.

Mark had not lived the life of a hermit, but his constant sales trips around the nation had left little time for a family—a fact attested to by his divorce a year and a half after marriage. Upon examining his net worth, he was pleasantly surprised. He had some $50,000 in CDs, $18,000 in a Super Now checking account and $72,000 in an income savings plan. He was, of course, nowhere near retirement and had no significant liabilities.

He did, however, have the dream of becoming an entrepreneur, of starting his own software company specializing in a database for used avionics equipment. Thus, his objective was to remain reasonably liquid for potential investment purposes while earning a decent short-term rate of return on his funds.

He cashed in his old CDs, which were paying only 6.25 percent, and removed all but a few months of living expenses from his Super Now, which paid only 5.85 percent. Furthermore, he closed his income savings plan when he left the company. In total, he had $135,000 to reposition.

Mark has earmarked $50,000 for his future business, knowing full well that no one would invest in his company unless he did as well. He has put these funds into short-term Treasury bills, which bring him 6.8 percent (free of state and local taxes). For the balance, Mark has divided it three ways: (1) as a true son of California, he has bought shares in a high-yielding real estate investment trust; (2) he has bought some common stock in a number of software companies with the sound belief that he knows his own industry best; and (3) he has bought stock in gold mining companies since he is convinced that when times of double-digit inflation return, the world will flock to gold. This combination of real estate, computers and gold makes him feel rather secure when he starts over again.

## PORTFOLIO 7: ENTREPRENEURS — BUSINESS AND INVESTING

At last count there were over 5 million self-employed individuals in the United States—probably the highest level of self-employment in the world. Arthur was one of them. A certified public accountant by training, he decided to leave the profession when one of his wealthy clients said (not "plastics") "semiconductors." This son of New York's City College reckoned that selling electronic components to the world could indeed be a path to wealth. He was tired of counting other people's money anyway.

From a Manhattan loft, he opened a sales organization, and before long his business was rolling. The level of taxes Arthur faced convinced him that there was ample room for a creative reduction. His plan was relatively simple: become a partnership. He soon managed to shift income from his high incorporated and personal levels to his wife and children, who enjoyed zero tax brackets.

Arthur knew that under the new tax code, incorporated businesses face a tax level of 34 percent, compared with the maximum rate on personal returns of 28 percent. Arthur also knew that his earnings would again be taxed after he paid corporate taxes—a clear form of double taxation. So he elected to become an "S" corporation—a business form that still gives liability protection but permits all income to be passed through to shareholders and taxed on a personal basis.

By giving each child and his wife a 10 percent interest in the business, Arthur knew that considerable sums would be saved by using their zero brackets. The potential for a gift tax was low since the gifts fall within the unified tax credit allowed to every donor.

Furthermore, Arthur has decided to set up investment programs for each family member, based roughly on the annual tax savings. Since he considers the savings as found money, he has invested in very aggressive growth securities, remembering that even capital losses are shared by the government.

## PORTFOLIO 8: SECOND FAMILIES AND SECOND MORTGAGES

The Census Bureau indicates that most Americans still believe in marriage; in fact, more than half of those divorced and widowed try again. Lila was about to try again after her first husband passed on. Her children were grown and out on their own, so no responsibilities existed there. When she became reacquainted with an old, single, high-school sweetheart, they agreed to marry.

Don, her new husband, decided that it was time for a change. A public relations consultant to oil and gas companies, Don thought it might be a time to try his own luck in the oil patch. In the early 1980s, he had bought a small series of stripper wells near Dallas, hoping to capitalize on the rise in oil prices. Don used a lot of borrowed money to finance the deal, but he had calculated a positive cash flow if oil remained at $24 a barrel.

For a couple of years his projections proved worthwhile. Based on that happy circumstance, he bought a large suburban home, again with a large mortgage, and finally a tract house with two rental units on the same terms. Don and Lila were maximizing the use of what can be a treacherous technique: pyramiding with credit. Of course, credit is the American way; however, they had not planned on any adverse contingencies. When oil prices fell and the tract house remained only half-rented, the dragon of negative cash flow raised its head.

To overcome what they considered a short-term event (the negative cash flow), they borrowed more money, but this time against their securities portfolio. Margin lending is one of the cheapest ways to borrow funds, and it does not have the paperwork hassle associated with ordinary bank loans. Don and Lila luckily had a blue-chip portfolio of quality companies plus some Treasury bonds.

The brokerage house was willing to lend up to 50 percent of the value of the common stock and up to 90 percent of the value of the government bonds. While the loan was considerably cheaper than other forms of borrowing or second mortgages, it did hold one danger—margin calls. If the value of the portfolio shrank dramatically, the broker would ask for more cash. Toward that contingency, they did not borrow to the hilt, leaving a considerable cushion.

The new tax code has made personal borrowing less advantageous since it limits tax deductibility, except in the case of homes and second homes. Nevertheless, borrowing funds slightly above the call money rate, as published in the daily press, certainly saves considerable sums over, say, a home equity loan. If the value of the underlying portfolio appreciates, the shares can be sold and the profits applied to the loan. The real question for Don and Lila is, When will oil prices turn up?

### PORTFOLIO 9: PREPARING FOR FINALS—TOWARD RETIREMENT

Warren and Rita moved from Chicago shortly after Warren's retirement as a machinist and part-owner of a repair shop. Their savings were ample if inflation did not heat up again, and they were taking down the maximum from Social Security. Nevertheless, it was important to keep a high cash flow, since as "snowbirds," they commuted twice a year from the Windy City. In addition, they had to maintain two residences.

Their major concern was the level of interest rates as they rolled over their CDs, mortgage obligations, tax-free municipals and junk bonds. They were forever calling their banks and brokerage house in search of the Holy Grail—

anything that offered double-digit returns. And that finally put them in hot water. The overreaching for yield can be a garden path in the wrong direction. Warren and Rita found out the hard way about risk-reward ratios.

They did indeed diversify, but with four kinds of fixed-interest instruments. They bought the longest-term CDs, since they typically pay the highest yields. But they found they were frozen into CDs when, because of family circumstances, they had to cash one in prematurely. The government requires a three-month interest penalty charge; some banks charge an even higher penalty, and others do not allow premature distribution at all.

Their second holding was a pool of pass-through mortgages. Again they reached for the highest yields, which meant that the funds were most vulnerable to interest rate fluctuations. They had bought the certificates near their high, but they suffered a loss of premium as mortgage holders refinanced their homes at lower rates. The government had guaranteed the principal but not the rate of interest.

The municipal bonds worked best for Warren and Rita because they produced steady, tax-free interest even when the principal fluctuated. It was the portfolio of junk bond funds that made them queasy, as the net asset value rose and fell like a roller coaster.

They omitted a few items in their retirement planning. They did not buy an annuity in case they outlived their savings and investments or if inflation simply made their living expenses more costly. The annuity, however, would have provided some additional funds if one of them lived far beyond actuarial expectations. In addition, it would have been wise to put some funds into dividend-paying growth equities. This would have increased the size of their assets, however modestly—a condition not available from a fixed-income portfolio.

## PORTFOLIO 10: SUNSET YEARS

Adele definitely did not have it all, her nephew Alfred reflected. Adele was now in her last decade, and probably in her last year. The senility had moved from the barely noticeable stage to the loss of motor control. It was an increasingly sad vision of a woman who had dressed herself in elegantly painstaking fashion at some of the city's better stores. Now there were racks and racks of dresses that were no longer seen, let alone worn.

Adele had had a great romance in her early thirties, but he was viewed as a poor choice by her parents. After all, one did not marry shopkeepers in those days. When the affair unhappily ended, Adele became a legal secretary, an occupation she was to follow for 40 years with the same firm. Adele's earnings mounted handsomely: she had no children to contribute to, no husband to support, an inexpensive rent-controlled apartment to live in and a law firm that amply rewarded her for her silence and flexibility.

Alfred became Adele's crutch in the sunset of her life, and she constantly relied on him for favors big and small. In turn, she made Alfred her heir apparent, having distanced herself from her remaining two sisters. As her Alzheimer's disease progressed, it became clear that she would soon need institutionalization.

When Alfred took charge of her affairs, he was dumbstruck by the size of her assets. The first thing he did was to obtain a general power of attorney to act in Adele's behalf. The document was available at a legal stationery store. While it was useful and necessary, Alfred found that, to his surprise, not everyone recognized the document. In fact, some banks demanded their own executed forms.

Adele clearly did not trust banks: she banked at 16 different banks. Whether it was because she had lived through the Great Depression, when so many banks failed, or whether it was the lure of toasters, VCRs or television sets, Alfred never found out.

In any event, he was faced with the monumental task of consolidating all those accounts into one or two accounts. Some of the accounts were passbooks, some were money market deposit accounts and some were CDs. For Alfred, the task was Herculean since he, like many consumers of financial services, suffered from bank tremens, a variant of delirium tremens. Instead of asking "Whose money is it anyway?" he was intimidated by insinuating bank officers.

Alfred faced two problems: (1) he had to consolidate 16 bank accounts, which totaled over half a million dollars; and (2) he had to have Adele admitted to a nursing home rather quickly. Unless he consolidated the accounts, he could never put her in the nursing home, as some homes require three months of fees up front.

There was one further consideration. Adele had accumulated that substantial estate not only to leave to heirs, but to have a nest egg for her old age. She had not counted on the vicious inflationary inroads and the skyrocketing costs of medical services. (The present confiscatory levels of nursing home rates are enough to empty most bank accounts.) Would she have enough for her final years, or would she be a welfare case in a few years? For the middle class, who save to pass on some inheritance to their children and grandchildren, it is often a nightmare, with children emptying bank accounts before Medicare and Medicaid authorities find out.

Would Adele be able to be maintained, or would all her funds be spent on her terminal illness? The first problem was solved when Alfred consulted his attorney, who suggested an inter vivos (or living) trust for Adele.

Alfred was appointed trustee for the Adele Trust, while Adele was the beneficiary as well as the grantor. All her property and the proceeds of the 16 bank accounts were placed in a trust account opened with a brokerage house. The purpose of trust was to maintain Adele in the nursing home. To that end, Alfred bought only utility, telephone and some bank stock, both common and preferred, with the balance in Treasury bills and money market funds. By investing for income and growth, he was able to generate more than sufficient funds to pay the nursing home. By using the inter vivos trust, the property would pass to Alfred without passing through the probate courts.

# • 15 •

## *How To Monitor Your Portfolio*

### THE NEED TO BE INVOLVED

Whether you are an active or passive investor, you have an obligation to be informed about economic and financial conditions. Active investors must certainly monitor general business affairs, plus specific news that has an impact on their investments. While passive investors may not wish to be so closely tied to the ebb and flow of daily, weekly or monthly information, they must have some overall understanding of what is happening to their money, what their objectives are, who is accountable to them, how decisions are made and what fees and commissions are being charged.

In short, you can no more leave your financial affairs totally to hired advisers, bank trust departments, investment management companies or even your neighborhood accountant than you can leave your health care to your physician. You must take some role in maintaining your health and monitoring your wealth.

Since you must be informed if you are to participate, what are the simplest and easiest ways to obtain meaningful market knowledge?

## WHERE CAN I GET INFORMATION?

*Daily Newspapers.* Newspapers are a must if you wish to keep abreast of current events. A good mix is a city or regional newspaper to cover local business news and *The Wall Street Journal* and/or *Investor's Business Daily* for the national markets. *The Wall Street Journal* is the establishment paper, and it is chock-full of fundamental information. *Investor's Business Daily* is relatively new and emphasizes technical trends. For global investors, the premier non-American English newspaper is *The Financial Times* of London.

*Daily Broadcasters.* Radio stations and nightly television news programs give spot news on business. Their presentations are, however, severely limited by the time constraints on the national networks. The Public Broadcasting System has a half-hour business news program, *The Nightly Business Report*, plus weekly programs by Adam Smith and Louis Rukeyser, devoted to timely economic matters. For cable viewers, CNBC/FNN maintains a running commentary on the securities markets, in addition to providing quotation tapes of current trades (delayed 15 minutes).

*Magazines.* While general news magazines devote some special sections to financial affairs, there are a number of magazines that specialize in business. The most popular ones are *Barron's, Business Week, Financial World, Forbes, Fortune* and *Money*. The premier magazine for an international perspective is *The Economist*. In addition, there are trade magazines for virtually every industry.

*Newsletters.* At last count, there were over 1,000 newsletters focusing on the securities markets. They range across every area—from common stocks to mutual funds, from bank credit analysis to Federal Reserve policies and from California municipal bonds to internationally defaulted sovereign state loans. The most popular newsletters are the publications of Babson-United, Moody's, Standard & Poor's and Value Line, along with the newsletters of some brokerage houses (for which even clients are charged a fee). Most newsletters recommend portfolios of securities, both through the mail and sometimes over a toll-free hot line. One newsletter, the *Hulbert Financial Digest*, rates more than 200 sample portfolios in 100 newsletters. Mark Hulbert, its founder, has observed that price should not be a consideration in selecting a newsletter as "there's no correlation whatsoever" between high prices of newsletters and high returns on investments.

***Primary Sources.*** Investors can obtain a company's annual report by requesting it from the company or through a brokerage house. The annual report is an abbreviated version (with pictures) of Form 10K, which must be filed annually with the Securities and Exchange Commission (SEC). The 10K gives a very complete report on the corporation's activities during the last fiscal year. Companies report their earnings quarterly through the media and to the SEC on Form 10Q, which investors can also obtain.

In addition to public relations releases (the company will put you on their distribution list if you so request), corporations occasionally meet with investment clubs, analyst societies and trade associations to report on their progress, along with holding annual general meetings. For new companies, the initial prospectus (sometimes called the "red herring") is must reading since it spells out degree of risk, competition, market share and financial underpinnings. An aggressive investor can also seek clarification directly from corporate officers, though they are often guarded in their responses for legal reasons.

***Data Bases.*** With the advent of the personal computer, a number of computerized data libraries can be accessed through telephone modem connections. This technique opens up stores of information about specific companies, industries, the economy, money markets and financial publications. Such services as CompuServe, Dialog (Predicast), Dow Jones, Genie, The Source and Standard & Poor's are wholesale vendors of their own and sometimes other competing financial services. There is a connection charge for all of the services, but the rates differ considerably, depending on when the service is used (prime or nonprime time) and the charge for each data base (from $5 to $150 per hour).

The research capabilities of the personal computer are awesome, as they tap into mainframe computers. Searches for financial information can move through contemporary and historical stories in the financial press, company analysis, charts, historical quotes, analysis and opinion, brokerage and investment banking house reports and legal inside trading, plus much more. The major compilers (as distinct from the vendors or distributors) are Dow Jones Retrieval, Disclosure, Investext, Media General, Moody's and Standard & Poor's. In addition, some investors subscribe to wire services, such as Knight Ridder, on their computers.

There are two other ways to access electronic information: (1) through the cable system and (2) through radio modems. Some financial publishers provide floppy discs with timely information that gives real-time information and analysis when tied to their cable systems. In a similar fashion, it is possible to use a radio modem connected to a personal computer to access current market quotations and other financial information. The data is broadcast over unused FM radio bands and is displayed on the monitor.

# WHAT INFORMATION IS
# WORTH MONITORING?

Unless you have a professional interest in the financial world, keeping abreast of the markets is a time-consuming business. And there is the very real danger that you may be inundated with irrelevant knowledge. Investors must make critical decisions on what is nice to know and what is necessary to know—and how to avoid the former while ensuring the acquisition of the latter.

The value of information is directly proportional to its impact on your investment. Or to put it another way, the value of market knowledge is only as relevant as what can be done with it. Thus, the state of the economy is worth considering, but there is not much that an individual can do about it. Moreover, the more general the information, the less relevance it is likely to have for a specific investment. The state of the economy is certainly important, but how does a citizen quantify that knowledge, and how does it affect his or her Treasury bonds or auto stocks?

To monitor the financial world, you as an investor should start with a broad, general understanding of the business cycle, governmental policies, Federal Reserve actions and the leading economic indicators. With this background, you can move on to a specific examination of sectors, industries and companies. This is generally considered a "top down" approach to the economic scene.

# WHAT IS A BUSINESS CYCLE?

It is of critical importance for investors and potential investors to know what stage of the business cycle they are currently in. For the last few hundred years, the business cycle has generally described the expansion and contraction of the whole economy. The cycle ranges in length from three to five years. It consists of five distinct phases: revival, expansion, maturation, contraction and recession.

After a recession, there is a period of revival. This is the initial phase of a business expansion where sales start to increase faster than anticipated. As profits rise and inventories shrink, the second phase—expansion—starts as business expands by accelerating production, hiring more workers and even increasing overtime. Income and profits continue to rise, causing businesses to expand even more, using up available plant capacity and showing enviable gains in productivity.

As the expansion feeds on itself, the cycle moves into its third phase—maturation—in which businesses increase prices, spending levels jump and bottlenecks develop. But in this maturation phase, consumers are reaching the limits of their spending capabilities (and/or the limits of their indebtedness), and they gradually pull back on consumption. Growth then ceases (two quarters of no growth indicate a recession, according to the National Bureau of Economic Research, the agency in charge of calling recessions), and the economy eases off and goes into a slump. In the fourth phase—contraction—inventory expands too rapidly, profit margins are squeezed, orders are soft and workers are laid off. The contraction in this fourth phase also feeds on itself as the economy slips into a rapid recession or bust, the final and last stage before a recovery begins again.

## HOW DOES THE CYCLE AFFECT STOCK PRICES?

There are no perfect correlations between the business cycle and stock prices since so many factors are involved—

from crowd psychology to fiscal policies. Moreover, it is hard to gauge how long a business cycle will last. Some cycles have gone full circle in a year and a half, but the average cycle is close to four years. The last business upturn celebrated its fifth anniversary just about the time the stock market crashed on Black Monday, October 19, 1987. One aspect seems true in modern times: expansions are longer than recessions since activist governmental policies move more quickly than before to shore up the economy. The public no longer tolerates high unemployment, plant closings or a prolonged recessionary environment.

While the job of the private National Bureau of Economic Research is to call a recession a recession, that, by its nature, is a retroactive call. Indeed, a recession is sometimes over by the time the Bureau has enough data to make that determination. Economists, business managers and financial observers cannot wait until after the fact to plot a course of action. The Department of Commerce keeps forecasting and understanding the state of the economy by issuing three sets of indicators: (1) leading, (2) coincident and (3) lagging.

The components of the leading indicators index are as follows:

1. Average workweek hours of manufacturing
2. Average weekly initial unemployment insurance claims
3. Manufacturers' new orders for consumer goods and materials
4. Standard & Poor's 500 composite index
5. Plant and equipment orders and contracts
6. Index of new private housing authorized by permit
7. Supplier delivery subcomponent of the purchasing managers index
8. University of Michigan index of consumer expectations
9. Net change in inventories on hand and on order

10. Change in sensitive materials price
11. Money supply: M2

These indicators are released monthly by the government, and while they occasionally give false signals, three back-to-back monthly declines are considered a precursor of recession.

The securities markets and business cycle watchers are especially concerned with the 11 components that make up the leading indicators since these separate series reach peaks and troughs before the economic activity of the business cycle.

Though it is hazardous to generalize, the business cycle has advantageous and disadvantageous times for investments. Remembering that timing is a key ingredient to all but the longest-term investor, the appropriateness of investment timing might be indicated by pluses and minuses (see Table 15.1).

## THE FEDERAL RESERVE SYSTEM AND ITS EFFECT ON INTEREST RATES

Investors are also obliged to examine the actions of the Federal Reserve System to determine how its policies are likely to affect the financial world. The "Fed" is the single, most important governmental agency to affect the economy. It plays this role by controlling a number of important spigots:

- The money supply
- The reserves available to the banking system
- The margin requirements for the securities markets
- Intervention in the foreign exchange markets
- Adjustments to the discount rate

**TABLE 15.1**  Business Cycle Investments

|             | *Stocks* | *Bonds* | *Gold/ Commodities* | *T-bills/Cash* |
|-------------|:--------:|:-------:|:-------------------:|:--------------:|
| Revival     | +        | +       |                     |                |
| Expansion   | +        | ?       | +                   | ?              |
| Maturation  | ?        |         | +                   | +              |
| Contraction |          |         | ?                   | +              |
| Recession   | +        | +       |                     | +              |

It is difficult to keep an eye on everything the Fed does since many of its actions are secret for a while or can only be read through conjecture. Twice a year the chairman of the Fed addresses Congress to set targets, but generalities are hard to interpret. For a number of years, the investment world scrutinized the money supply report the Fed issued weekly, looking for a clue as to whether expansion beyond expectations was inflationary or whether a contraction of the monetary aggregates indicated a tightening of credit. As *monetarism* (the belief that a steady control and an even supply of money keep the economy in equilibrium) has lost some of its political appeal, the pendulum has swung back to concern over the discount rate, the federal funds rate and the foreign exchange markets. (The *discount rate* is the rate the Fed charges to banks forced to borrow from the central bank; the *federal funds rate* is the rate banks charge each other to borrow excess reserves.)

Regardless of which fad is currently in fashion, both the money supply and the discount rate are two obvious and critical benchmarks for the Fed. By manipulating them, the Fed attempts to keep the economy on an even keel. But the Fed occasionally leans the wrong way at the wrong time; its movements are not a perfect predictor of future economic or investment decisions.

Nevertheless, the actions of the Fed should be scrutinized with care since they may lead to major market turns. For example, the day after the October meltdown in 1987, when the markets were in great disarray, the Fed stepped in with a brief one-sentence assurance that it would supply all the liquidity the investment world would need to overcome its panic. The very next day the markets rallied and some confidence returned.

Most moves by the Fed are far less dramatic. In general, a series of discount rate rises will indicate tighter credit and an attempt to cool an overheated economy in the expansion or maturation stage of the business cycle. For bond investors, this is a warning that interest rates are rising and bond prices are falling. Equity investors will find a note of caution if money starts to become tight and costly. An old proverb sums it up: Three steps and a stumble. When the discount rate is raised three times in a row, the stock market is likely to fall. As with all rules of thumb, it must be taken in context.

So, too, with the monetary aggregates, or money supply. It is not so much the actual increase or decrease of the money supply, but the extent to which the weekly figures deviate from the announced targets. If the rate of growth is consistently too high, the Federal Open Market Committee (FOMC) will move to reduce growth by selling Treasury paper in the market. Conversely, if supply falls below the targets, the Fed will supply funds by buying Treasury securities. In the former case, interest rates are likely to be nudged upward, and in the latter, they will tilt downward.

One of the primary policy concerns of the Federal Reserve System is to keep inflation under control. If inflation is getting out of hand with indications that the monetary aggregates are too high and above target, the Fed will move more insistently to cut the flow. This is a bearish sign for equity investors but a bullish one for bondholders if interest rates start to fall. On the other hand, if supply is consistently below target, the stock market is likely to be content with easy credit, though some bondholders will find that worrisome.

Some observers have claimed that predicting interest rates is equivalent to forecasting the weather—but without the benefit of knowing what season it is. Most economists and financial observers have egg on their face from trying, but by watching the Fed's action, one can have some idea of the immediate situation and perhaps get a glimpse into the immediate future. The central bank can influence near-term interest rates but must contend with public opinion, both here and abroad, in steering long-term rates.

Of late, the United States has had to contend with pressures from overseas in its financial markets. To cover our massive federal deficit and trade imbalance, the Treasury borrows huge amounts at its continuing auctions. To keep foreign buyers of American debt happy, the government has had to walk a tightrope. Since early in 1985 the dollar has lost nearly half its value against many major currencies.

Foreign investors are not very ready to buy dollar-denominated bonds if they face currency depreciation. Thus, the Fed has had attempted to keep the dollar from falling too low (even if that action served to help the export sector and the trade balance), while keeping interest rates sufficiently high to attract foreign funds. All the while, the Fed has to pay attention to its domestic constituency, realizing full well that if interest rates are too high, credit will evaporate and a recession is sure to follow. Interest rates are now tied to the global economy in a way never previously envisioned.

Investors must take into account all these factors in deciding where the economy is in the business cycle and where it is likely to go in the face of not only economic but political uncertainty. There are no simple answers to these complicated issues. Investors and potential investors should hedge their options for a safe haven. To do nothing invariably invites loss of capital and reduced purchasing power in the inflationary years ahead. For investors, some combination of equity ownership, fixed-income securities and informed speculation is likely to prove most beneficial, as it has in the past. The other three volumes in this series—*The Basics of Stocks, The Basics of Bonds* and *The Basics of Speculating*—will help to chart that course as well as provide some strategic and tactical advice on how to achieve your objectives.

## Y·O·U·R   M·O·V·E

- Active investors must monitor portfolio holdings, if not daily, at least weekly. Aggressive portfolios call for constant vigilance. Passive or extraordinarily conservative investors need to review their portfolios only quarterly.

- Business cycles are a major determinant in the movement of stock prices. Try to assess the economy and look for clues as to the present situation and future trends. Markets are anticipatory mechanisms: they are always evaluating what will happen in six months or a year.

- New portfolio selections should be made not only on their basic financial facts but with an eye on how a choice will fit into the economic picture next year. You do not want to buy long-term savings instruments if the economy is faced with strong inflationary forces. Conversely, you would certainly want to consider bonds in the face of a deflationary period.

- Action of the Federal Reserve System is paramount in determining interest rates. If you see the discount, prime or federal funds rates gradually rise, the economy is being reined in and equity markets are likely to suffer. Rising interest rates depress bonds as bondholders fear a new round of inflation.

- Pay attention to the global strength of the dollar. The Fed must keep interest rates relatively high to attract buyers of U.S. government obligations. That action strengthens the dollar but hurts the export industries. If the dollar weakens dramatically, foreign buyers may be reluctant to buy U.S. assets and may even withdraw their funds. A flight from the dollar might spell serious trouble for U.S. markets.

# *Epilogue*

The necessity of saving and investing should be clear to anyone concerned with his or her financial future in a period of uncertainty and volatility. Financial assets give you and your family a strong bargaining position in your job and career, the freedom to pursue a more desirable life-style, cultural amenities, material advantages and a comfortable old age. We all have our own set of priorities, but all our needs are more apt to be met with money in the bank.

Saving should be an important part of your financial life. If you start by saving 5 percent or more of your disposable income early in life, you should continue this practice throughout your working career. Whatever you save, put that money to work at the highest rate of interest, preferably in instruments with long maturities. Your involuntary savings (such as life insurance, your home mortgage, etc.) will take care of themselves.

The third leg of your financial plan should be an investment program. When your personal savings reach $20,000 or one year's earnings (whichever is greater), it is time to consider stocks and bonds seriously.

An investment program will increase the rate of return on your funds far faster than any savings program. Exactly how much more an investment program will yield is impossible to say. The stock market has historically returned over 9 percent (before dividends) to long-term investors. In recent years (the 1980s), the return has been even higher. That historical average (with dividends) is more than 100 percent above the rate of return on passbook savings. Moreover, there may well be additional tax advantages in municipal bond income, and investing through pension and retirement accounts.

You don't need a lot of money to start an investment program. Perhaps the simplest way to start is with an open-end mutual fund. If you wish to go no further as an investor, consider other funds with the objectives of income, government-guaranteed obligations or tax-free income. There are virtually a dozen categories of funds—from special sector funds to foreign country funds—to meet your goals.

It is important for you to be certain what level of risk you wish to tolerate. In selecting a fund or an investment advisor, you will stay out of the wrong situations if you understand your own risk tolerances.

One of the great benefits of mutual funds is that you don't need a great deal of money to invest since share prices are relatively low. If you wish to become more active, you must use discipline and discretion in selecting a balanced portfolio. To accomplish that, be ready to invest at least $5,000 to $10,000. By buying half a dozen or so issues over a period of time, you will reduce your exposure to untoward events—risks you cannot foretell or control.

If your portfolio grows profitably, consider investing additional funds on a regular basis—just as you do with savings. By looking at your own net worth statement, you may decide to reallocate some of your funds to purchase securities. Moreover, you might also consider borrowing funds (margin) against the value of your invested securities. Credit is a powerful tool to increase the return on your assets.

The universe of securities is enormous. Your job is to select a diversified group to complement your goals. There is risk in the stock and bond markets. The way to hedge that risk is to balance your portfolio. Whether you are investing for income or growth (you are likely to have a little of each in a rounded portfolio), it is wise to consider the whole range of investment securities.

There are 200 industrial categories and 50,000 companies with tradable securities in the United States. The prices of these issues rise and fall in relation to interest rates and the business cycle. By paying close attention to the actions of the Federal Reserve System as it manipulates interest rates, as well as the conditions of the economy, you will develop a strong sense of why prices move as they do. You will then be able to enter and exit the markets at the most favorable times.

If, on the other hand, you believe that there is no correlation between business conditions and securities' prices, you will find it difficult to make market decisions. The markets are not totally predictable, but you are in a far stronger position to profit if you come armed with information and knowledge. History may not precisely repeat itself, but market patterns are repleat with similar variations on a theme.

Since it is not given to investors (or anyone else) to foresee economic developments, it is important to be prepared for all contingencies. The next three books in this series concentrate on the stock market, the fixed-income or bond market and the speculative world of commodities and derivative instruments. You will then be ready for any economic conditions as you bank and build financial assets for the future.

# *Glossary*

**assets**  Anything of value owned by an individual or company. An asset may be a specific property or simply a legitimate claim against others.

**at the money**  The exercise price of an option is equal to the price of its underlying shares.

**bearer bond**  A bond that does not have the owner's name registered on its face or on the books of the issuer. The person having a bearer bond in his or her possession is considered to be the owner. Interest and principal are payable to the holder, and no endorsement is required on transfers. Although tax law changes enacted in 1982 effectively prohibit the issuance of new bonds in bearer form, already outstanding bearer bonds may be purchased in secondary markets.

**beta**  A mathematic measurement of a stock's sensitivity to the movement of the general market. A beta of 1 means that the stock moves in line with the market, but a beta of 1.5 means that it is 50 percent more volatile on the up side than the general market.

**blue chips**  A generic description given to the largest, well-capitalized corporations, such as IBM.

**bond**  A secured promissory note that represents the issuer's pledge to pay back the principal at face value on a specific date. Until that date, the issuer generally agrees to pay a fixed amount of interest at six-month intervals. The term *bond* frequently is applied to other types of fixed-income instruments that technically are not bonds at all.

**business cycle**   The alternating phases of business conditions that range from boom to bust. A typical business cycle has five phases: revival, expansion, maturation, contraction and recession.

**calls**   A call option gives the buyer the right to buy 100 shares of the underlying stock at a stated price at any time before the option expires.

**capital gain (loss)**   The profit (or loss) from the sale of an investment or capital asset above (or below) the purchase price.

**certificate of deposit (CD)**   A type of interest-bearing debt instrument that is issued by banking institutions.

**closed-end fund**   A mutual fund with a limited number of shares, frequently traded on a listed stock exchange.

**common stock**   Shares of a corporation representing the ownership interest. Common stock has a junior claim on earnings, dividends and assets compared to preferred issues and bonds.

**company risk**   Business conditions are always uncertain, and all corporations are subject to the vicissitudes of their markets. Investors in the corporate bond market may find their investments affected by business conditions even though they are creditors, not owners.

**consumer price index (CPI)**   A measurement of the cost of living for the public published by the Bureau of Labor Statistics.

**conversion price**   The price at which a convertible bond (or preferred stock) can be exchanged for the common stock of a corporation.

**convertible bond**   A bond that gives its holder the privilege of exchanging it for common stock of the issuing corporation on a preferred basis at some later date.

**current yield**   The percentage return on a bond calculated by dividing the annual interest payments by the present price of the bond. For example, a 13 percent par value bond of $1,000 selling at $950 offers a current yield of 13.7 percent ($130 ÷ $950 = 13.7 percent).

**debenture**   An unsecured, long-term debt obligation issued by a corporation. The debenture is issued against the general credit of the corporation, rather than against a specific asset.

**debt securities** Any of the large class of fixed-income securities that are essentially forms of corporate IOUs. They all pay some interest (except for zeros and those in default), and they all have specific priorities in terms of their credit seniority.

**deep discount bond (original issue)** An issue of bonds sold at a deep discount from its par value. The coupon rate is low compared to prevailing interest rates.

**default** Failure to perform a contractual obligation, particularly the payment of interest or principal on debt at a stated date.

**derivative instruments** Securities that obtain much of their value from related or underlying securities or commodities. Their prices depend on the price of the underlying issues.

**discount rate** The rate the Federal Reserve System charges to member banks for loans. It is a rate that the Fed changes to tighten and ease monetary conditions.

**disinflation** A decline in the rate of inflation.

**dividends** A distribution of company earnings to the stockholders.

**Dow Jones Industrial Average** An indicator of 30 leading blue chips published by the Dow Jones Publishing Company.

**effective yield** This is the actual yield on an investment after allowing for compounding over a period of time, in contrast to the nominal or stated rate.

**equity** The common stock of a corporation. Also the net worth of a corporate balance sheet and/or the net balance in a brokerage account.

**federal funds rate** The interest rate charged by banks on their excess reserve funds to banks that are deficient in their reserve positions.

**Federal Reserve System** The central banking system of the United States. It has many functions, but perhaps the chief function is to regulate the amount of credit in the national economy.

**fixed-income investment** Any debt obligation that returns to the investor or depositor a set sum (interest) on a regular basis, whether it be monthly, quarterly, semiannually or annually. This broad category encompasses time deposits in banks, money market instruments (such as commercial paper issued by corporations), money market accounts and/or funds and bonds. The term also applies to bonds (such as zero coupon bonds) and CDs that pay interest at maturity or at the end of their terms.

**general obligation bond (GO)**   A bond issued by a state or political subdivision that is backed by the full faith and credit (taxing power) of the issuer.

**high-yielding bond**   A debt obligation that provides a rate of interest far exceeding average rates of return. These are almost always speculative bonds and have high rates of default. They are commonly referred to as "junk" bonds, but there are hundreds of these issues. Some are better than others.

**inflation**   An increase in the price level that in turn results in a decrease in purchasing power.

**initial margin requirement**   The amount of money required to establish a margin account. This figure is set by the Federal Reserve System.

**interest**   The price paid for borrowed funds, the rent for money.

**interest rate risk**   The fluctuations of capital caused by the rise and fall of interest rates. The inverse relationship of principal to interest rates means that when interest rates rise, principal falls, and vice versa. All negotiable fixed-income investments are subject to interest rate risk.

**in the money**   A call is in the money when the underlying shares are selling above the exercise price. A put is in the money when the underlying shares are selling below the strike price.

**junk bond**   *See* high-yielding bond.

**leverage**   The relationship of corporate debt to equity can effect earnings when a significant amount of earnings must be paid to service bond interest or preferred stock dividends. Should a corporation earn a return on the borrowed money above the cost of the debt, leverage is successful. This will increase the return on the common stock without additional investment. If the leverage is unsuccessful, it will decimate earnings and leave little if anything to the stockholder. The use of credit in a margin account is a form of leverage.

**liabilities**   All the claims against a person or corporation.

**liquidity** The ability of a business to change its assets into cash without any loss. Measurements of liquidity attest to a corporation's health. In the securities market, liquidity is the ability to transact purchases and sales without any significant concession in price.

**load** A sales charge levied by an investment company for the purchase of its mutual funds.

**long position** This describes the ownership of common stock in the anticipation of an increase in price.

**margin** The use of a brokerage firm's credit to purchase securities. For the accommodation, the broker charges interest.

**market risk** All businesses (and governmental bonds to some degree) are affected by systemwide events in the economy. It is difficult to define exactly what constitutes market risk, but some past examples include a crash in the stock market, a presidential assassination or an act of war—events that had national or global ramifications.

**maturity** The date at which a debt obligation must be repaid by the issuer.

**money market account** A demand deposit bank account that pays interest comparable to money market instruments such as commercial paper, bankers' acceptances and Treasury bills.

**money market fund** A type of mutual fund that specializes in investments in short-term debt instruments, including government paper, commercial paper issued by corporations and bank CDs.

**mortgage-backed security** A certificate issued by either a public agency or a private corporation that is backed by a pool of residential or commercial mortgages. Interest and principal are passed through to the certificate owners on a monthly basis.

**mutual fund** Also known as an open-end investment company, the mutual fund invests the pooled cash of numerous investors in a managed portfolio designed to meet the fund's stated objectives. Mutual funds generally stand ready to sell and redeem their shares at any time at the current net asset value per share.

**negotiable instrument** Any security that can be freely exchanged for money, such as a stock, bond, check or draft.

**net asset value (NAV)**    All of the assets of a mutual fund minus all of the liabilities. The net asset value is frequently expressed on a per-share basis.

**net worth**    For an individual, the net worth is calculated by deducting all liabilities from the total value of personal assets.

**no-load fund**    A mutual fund that does not impose a sales charge or commission on its shares. Some funds are back-loaded, that is, they charge no sales charge on purchase but charge a fee if the purchaser sells the shares before a given period of years.

**note**    A debt obligation, usually unsecured and frequently with a maturity of five years or less at the time of issue.

**odd lot**    An order for a limited number of shares, but for less than 100, which is a round lot.

**open-end fund**    A mutual fund that continuously sells and repurchases its shares at the net asset value.

**option**    A right sold by one party to another for a premium to buy (a call option) or sell (a put option) a security at a fixed price during a specific period of time.

**over-the-counter (OTC) market**    A broker-dealer market operated totally through telephone and television communications. The OTC market is largely the home of low-priced, unseasoned securities. Some major companies, such as Apple Computer, prefer this unlisted market to the exchanges.

**preferred stock**    Stock that has a prior claim to a corporation's earnings, dividends and assets over the common stock, but behind the bonds. Dividends are frequently cumulative, that is, if they are not paid when due.

**premium**    The cost for transacting an option agreement.

**put**    An option to sell a security at a fixed price during a stated period of time.

**rate of return**    The yield obtained on an investment based on its purchase price.

**refunding bond**    A bond issued to retire another bond outstanding.

**registered bond**    A bond that has the name of its owners or the owner's agent written on its face and recorded on the books of the issuer. Ownership may be transferred only by the owner or agent.

**repurchase agreement (REPO, RP)** An arrangement in which a lender lends a bank funds for a short period. The bank in turn promises to repay the lender principal and interest at maturity. Repurchase agreements are more liquid than CDs and do not entail a penalty for early withdrawal.

**return on investment (ROI)** *See* rate of return.

**revenue bonds** Bonds issued by a government or agency. The revenue from the specific activity (e.g., a port authority) is used to pay off the bondholders.

**reverse home mortgage** A reverse mortgage issued to a homeowner who would like to withdraw equity from his or her home on a monthly basis. The bank eventually owns the property and takes possession upon a move or death.

**risk** A condition in the investment world that precludes a predictable or certain outcome. In fixed-income investments, some instruments are risk-free, such as U.S. government obligations and time deposits in banks, while the rest contain some element of chance. The amount of risk is measured by the rating agencies. In the stock market, virtually all investments have some risk, that is, the outcome of the investment is uncertain. Risk, of course, means the possibility of loss of funds.

**risk averse** Risk-averse investors wish to avoid chancy situations and the possibility of loss. They insist on knowing the interest rate, the yield and the maturity or redemption date.

**risk lover** Some investors welcome chance since it implies greater than average rewards.

**risk neutral** Risk-neutral investors neither welcome risk nor shun it. They are willing to tolerate some level of chance in the return on their investment portfolios.

**round lot** One hundred shares of common stock.

**secondary market** For fixed-income investments, the bond markets that facilitate trades after the original issue has been underwritten by investment bankers (e.g., the New York Stock Exchange, the American Stock Exchange or the OTC market).

**senior securities** Bonds and preferred issues that receive consideration before common stock in case of a bankruptcy or other financial difficulties.

**Standard & Poor's 500** A broad-based index of 500 companies published by the Standard & Poor's Corporation.

**stripped Treasuries** Zero coupon bonds that are based or formulated on Treasury bonds with their interest coupons removed. The U.S. Treasury also issues its own generic brand of stripped instruments.

**Treasury bill** A debt obligation of the U.S. government with a maturity of 52 weeks or less from the date of issue. T-bills are sold at a discount, and your return is the difference between the purchase price and the face value that is repaid at maturity.

**Treasury bond** A long-term debt obligation of the U.S. government having a maturity of seven years or more from the date of issue. Interest is at a fixed rate, payable semiannually.

**Treasury note** A U.S. government debt obligation with a maturity of not less than one or more than seven years from the date of issue. Otherwise, it is identical to a Treasury bond.

**underwriter** Also known as an investment banker, the underwriter is a middleman between corporations or municipalities issuing new securities and the individuals or institutions to which the issue is sold. The underwriter is responsible for the ultimate sale of the issue and either buys the whole issue and resells it to investors or forms a group to sell the bonds.

**unit investment trust** A vehicle sponsored by brokerage firms that invest the pooled funds of many investors in a fixed portfolio of interest-bearing securities. Units usually can be purchased for $1,000.

**warrant (WT)** A certificate giving the holder a right to purchase the common stock of a corporation at a fixed price within a specified period of time. Warrants are usually issued with debt issues as an enticement to buy senior securities.

**yield** The rate of return received from an investment and usually expressed annually.

**yield curve**   The graphic representation of interest rates (usually for Treasury securities) over a period of time—from tomorrow to 30 years.

**yield to maturity (YTM)**   The yield on a bond, taking into consideration the price paid, the interest to be received and the principal amount to be repaid at maturity.

**zero coupon bond**   A deep discount bond that bears no coupons. The return is based on the difference between the purchase price and the principal amount repaid at maturity.

# *Index*